The
EYES
of the
HEART

Books by Tracie Peterson

www.traciepeterson.com

Controlling Interests
Entangled • *Framed*
The Long-Awaited Child
A Slender Thread • *Tidings of Peace*

DESERT ROSES
Shadows of the Canyon

WESTWARD CHRONICLES
A Shelter of Hope • *Hidden in a Whisper*
A Veiled Reflection

RIBBONS OF STEEL*
Distant Dreams • *A Hope Beyond*
A Promise for Tomorrow

RIBBONS WEST*
Westward the Dream • *Separate Roads*
Ties That Bind

SHANNON SAGA†
City of Angels • *Angels Flight*
Angel of Mercy

YUKON QUEST
Treasures of the North • *Ashes and Ice*
Rivers of Gold

NONFICTION
The Eyes of the Heart

*with Judith Pella   †with James Scott Bell

The
EYES
of the
HEART

TRACIE PETERSON

BETHANY HOUSE PUBLISHERS
Minneapolis, Minnesota

Published by Bethany House Publishers
A Ministry of Bethany Fellowship International
11400 Hampshire Avenue South
Bloomington, Minnesota 55438
www.bethanyhouse.com

Printed in the United States of America by
Bethany Press International, Bloomington, Minnesota 55438

Library of Congress Cataloging-in-Publication Data

Peterson, Tracie.
    The eyes of the heart : seeing God's hand in the everyday moments of life / by Tracie Peterson.
      p. cm.
    ISBN 0-7642-2520-0 (pbk.)
    1. Christian women—Prayer-books and devotions—English.
2. Meditations. I. Title.
    BV4844 .P48   2002
    242—dc21

                               2002007786

TRACIE PETERSON is a popular speaker and bestselling author who has written over fifty books, both historical and contemporary fiction. Tracie and her family make their home in Montana.

Visit Tracie's Web site at: *www.traciepeterson.com.*

Contents

I pray also that the eyes of your

heart may be enlightened in order

that you may know the hope to

which he has called you, the riches

of his glorious inheritance in the

saints, and his incomparably great

power for us who believe.

EPHESIANS 1:18–19

Introduction

As a child I always thought people saw life the same way. I thought boys, girls, men, women, everyone had the same gifts and vision for the world around them. I was wrong. As I grew up, both spiritually and physically, I came to see the uniqueness of each individual. I don't think this lesson was driven home any more clearly than when my sister, Karen, commented to me that she couldn't string two words together and have them make sense.

How could this be? I thought. Didn't everyone possess the desire to write—and the ability? I figured writing was one of those original three basics you learned in school; how could she stand there and tell me she didn't have what it took to do this? Gradually I heard other people say the same thing. And silly as it sounds, that was when I came to better understand that God's gifts and the talents He gives are uniquely designed for the person He desires us to be.

With this in mind, the concept for this book was born. I came to realize that some people find it easy to see God in everyday life, while others struggle with the burdens they carry, unable to see much of anything. Sometimes obstacles keep them from seeing the truth. And sometimes the truth is the very last thing they want to see.

Having been in both places, it has become my desire to share with you how God opened the eyes of my heart. I want to share this, because these lessons changed my life. And like a very special party where everyone is going to have a marvelous time, I didn't want you to miss out.

So settle back and view the world through my eyes, if you will. Open your heart to the wonder of God's picture lessons. Let the eyes of your heart be enlightened that you might have hope. Hope that comes not from a book, or from me, for we will both fade away to dust. No, let the hope come from the King of the Universe, who loves you now even as He loved you on the cross.

Oh, and by the way, my sister, Karen, has a marvelous ability with numbers. She can do algebraic expressions in her sleep—a talent God did not see fit to bless me with. Unique in the Lord? You bet. Ah, the wonder of God!

—Tracie

1

The Consequences of Our Actions

One August afternoon I happened to be at the airport waiting for a flight. I sat watching the people around me, one of my favorite hobbies, and noted a scene that has stayed with me in a haunting manner ever since.

To one side of the waiting area, a woman stood with two children. A boy, who looked to be around twelve, maybe thirteen, and a girl no older than ten stood laden with backpacks and sweaters, clearly caught up in conversation with the woman. Off to the left, nearly ten or twelve feet away, stood a man most intent on the situation, but clearly alienated. For whatever reason, he wasn't being allowed to share in this farewell, although I could tell quite easily that he had some part in this strange little drama.

But what really held my attention, in fact, made me feel like the intruder I was, were the tears of the woman and the young girl. They weren't merely crying, they were sobbing. It was a heart-wrenching sob, the kind that reaches the center of your soul and permeates your body. The boy was trying so hard to be stoic, but I could see his lip quivering as the woman spoke to him.

Tenderly she reached out and touched their faces, and I knew then that she had to be their mother. No one touches a child in quite the same way as a mother does, especially one with deep emotional ties. She cried, touched them again, hugged them close, and then pulled away to try to speak again. They clung to her and she to them. And all the while the man only watched. As did I.

The flight was called, and I saw her face—the sheer look of anguish and something akin to panic. She pulled the children close, and I heard her sob even louder as she told them she loved them. The little girl was clearly devastated. So was the boy. I saw the open wounds of his heart written on his face.

An airline representative came forward. She smiled sympathetically, assuring the woman that she would see to the children. She led them away after the woman was allowed one final kiss, one final embrace. The two looked over their shoulders as the uniformed woman escorted them to the plane. The woman reached out her hand to wave good-bye—to fill the space that now separated them.

And then they were gone.

The man came forward, and the distraught woman collapsed in his arms. Everyone was watching by now. The scene mesmerized us all. What had just happened here? Why was this woman being separated from the children she so obviously loved?

I watched her walk to the long wall of windows. She pressed her hand to the glass as if she could somehow touch them again. The man stood behind her, stroking her shoulder. Her heart was on that plane, and he seemed to understand quite well.

I struggled with the timing of the situation. It was already late August. Time for school. These children were obviously headed out, away from their mother, for a good long while. After all, who would put school-aged children on a plane for a vacation at that time of the year? Besides, from the pained expressions and sobbing, these children weren't on a simple trip to Grandma's house. They were leaving home.

Of course, I have no idea who they were or where they were headed. I don't know why the little family was being torn apart. Perhaps the children lived with their father. Obviously the man who comforted the woman had a very small role in their lives. He hadn't come forward before they left. Hadn't even so much as waved good-bye.

It's impossible for me to know with certainty exactly what their situation was, but I do know that their pain came as a result of previous actions.

Sometimes it's easy to make a choice or a decision. We give it a halfhearted going over, certain that we have seen all the possible consequences or side effects.

Anger may drive us to reject someone who loves us. Rebellion sends us down a path we know better than to go. Anticipation of pleasure or temporary reward beckons us forward without regard to the cost.

We often make choices based on emotions and half-thought-out commentary. We think ourselves rather clever for having "given it over to God." When, in fact, we haven't given it honest consideration or a reasonable time to be worked through. And have we really given it to God?

Think about the last time you had a truly hard choice to make—about the moment you first became uncomfortable with the matter. Did you start rationalizing to be rid of that feeling? Did you quickly sweep the problem under the rug, even at the expense of hurting someone?

Did you tell everyone how you were deliberating over all the possible solutions, when, in fact, you'd made up your mind in the first five minutes as to how you were going to solve the problem? Was any consideration given to the consequences of your actions?

Consequences come along after the fact. Sometimes they're good, like when you apply for a job and get the call that you got it. New employment is a consequence of your action. Maybe you've performed a genuine act of kindness or generosity. The consequence could be anything from a warm fuzzy feeling inside to public recognition. Maybe the act was done in total anonymity, and the consequence is another jewel in your crown.

Consequences can also be bad, quite often tragic. A carload of teenagers decides to go drinking . . . and driving. An accident occurs, and several are killed. A young mother leaves her child alone at the pool—just long enough to answer the telephone, but also long enough for the child to drown. Or maybe it's nothing so dramatic as that. Maybe it's as simple as growing tired of a marriage that is laden with problems. A divorce seems like an amicable solution. But there are kids in the middle, and airport good-byes will come later.

I wonder if our choices would be different if we could see a video of the consequences prior to making our choice. Maybe angry words would go unsaid if we could see past our choice to the painful effect of our words. Maybe one less door would be slammed shut, one less selfish choice imposed, if we knew the outcome.

Maybe more positive choices would be made if we could see the consequences ahead of time. Maybe we'd be more aware of those around us if we could see ahead to the joy a Christmas basket would give an old man who lives alone. If we knew our kind words and patient listening gave a grieving neighbor hope, we might try more often to be a bearer of comfort. If we could watch that video and see the choice we had to speak in harshness or say nothing at all, we might recognize that silence is sometimes golden.

It seems a simple task to stop long enough to think ahead, to see down the road to the consequences of our choice. Picture yourself in an airport, saying good-bye to a child who doesn't understand the pain she is suffering.

There were consequences on the way to the cross. There were consequences on the cross. These gave us hope in the same hour that they struck others with despair. Jesus knew the consequences of being the Son of God. He knew the choices to be made; He knew by looking past the initial problems what would be the outcome of those choices.

Sometimes we need to look at the bigger picture. We need to look past the cross to understand that we wield a tremendous amount of power in our everyday choices and decisions. Jesus looked past the cross. He played out the video and saw the beatings, the humiliation, and the desertion. He knew what He faced, but He saw something else—He saw you and me.

He saw your loneliness and your sorrow. He saw you being falsely accused and unjustly condemned. He saw you at the airport, sobbing as you said good-bye to your children.

And when the video was done, He knew the horror of the cross would be worth it. He knew you would need Him to be there in your place. The consequence of His act was love—eternal and secure, evident and real. Aren't you glad He looked beyond the choices?

2

The Influence of Time

I'm always amazed when I look at the stages of growth in the lives of my children. It seems just yesterday they were small and helpless. I held them and nurtured them, talked to them and played with them. I dreamed of what they would grow up to be. I wondered if they would make good choices or bad ones. Would they listen to my advice or set it aside for something more popular?

I look at my children now and see the influence of time. When they were very small they were easily entertained with a book. When they reached preschool age, they were fascinated by television—particularly cartoons. Soon possessions became something of increasing concern. We worked to teach them that people were more deserving of their attention. We made gallant strides to entertain and to teach from methods other than television and the latest action figure.

By the time they were eight or nine, cartoons were losing

interest, and teenage crisis shows and sitcoms were the star attractions. There were shows where kids had special powers, special friends, and special problems. We listened to comical one-liners, where kids were always smarter than their parents, and watched conflict and poor choices work themselves out in thirty minutes. Everywhere you went, the influence was there. Slick designer clothes with the images of characters from movies and television shows. Toys with clear, concise themes that directed you back to the characters of the most popular TV series, so that even when you managed to limit the hours of viewing, you found the same themes in a variety of forms: anything from food in the grocery store to shoes on your child's feet. Imagine my surprise when I went to buy a simple pair of tennis shoes for my nine year old and couldn't find anything without a current theme.

My teenagers were given over to the latest craze among their own age group. Who has not yet memorized the zip code of that very important posh suburb of Los Angeles? Whether you allowed the show to be seen or not, you certainly were inundated with the essence of its characters. Then came the strong appeal to being frightened. Horror movies and gut-wrenching (or is that retching) thrillers with body parts flying and more blood spilled than during both World Wars. The influence of time was not kind. It was scary.

I can't tell you the number of times I've heard folks say, "This is just a rite of passage." A sort of modern-day coming of age.

But time has a way of moving on, and of leaving us behind in its wake. We see ourselves in the middle of life much like a two-bit player in a bad theatrical production. Never quite knowing our lines. Never quite sure how we're doing.

The other day I came across the verse in Luke 2:52: "And Jesus grew in wisdom and stature, and in favor with God and men."

During His time on earth, Jesus grew in wisdom. Wisdom that told Him what it was to be human—to feel joy and sorrow, to know pain and comfort. Wisdom gave Him a heart for intercession. When He sits at the right hand of God, speaking to the Father on our behalf, He knows what we are going through.

"Father, there's this special woman down there. She's lonely and she needs a mate. She's asking for just the right man—she's seen what the wrong partner can mean to a marriage. She's faithful and hopeful, as you know, but Father, I know what it is to feel lonely. To feel that no one cares if you come or go. To realize that there's no one waiting up for you, that there's no one to talk to."

He grew in stature too: height, weight, body mass. All that changed as Jesus the boy grew into Jesus the man. Maybe He felt gangly and awkward in His adolescent years. Maybe puberty was just as confusing and frustrating for Jesus as it is for every other teenager.

Or maybe stature meant a level of achievement. He learned His Torah. He memorized the Scriptures and laws given by His Father long before the fulfillment of the Messiah—Scriptures and laws Jesus the Creator was well aware of, but Jesus the man was expected to study and develop an understanding for. How strange the influence of time must have been for him.

He grew in favor with God and man. Both of His fathers—His heavenly one to whom He was so intricately bound, His earthly one to whom He was ever compared. "That's a good job, son," Joseph no doubt said, eyeing his son's carpentry work. "Joseph's boy has done some real fine work," the people of the village would have murmured.

"This is my son, in whom I am well pleased," said the heavenly voice of God.

The influence of time set Jesus upon His course. It gave Him purpose and showed Him the often hidden, intricate details that change lives.

He met a Samaritan woman by the well and told her about the living water. He healed the blind and restored lepers. He heard a father's plea for a dying child and the mournful cry of two sisters for a brother who had died before Jesus got to their house. And on the way to Calvary, He took that influence, the paths He traveled, the lives He'd changed, and remembered each one as He was nailed to a cross He didn't deserve.

BAM! The hammer drove the nails.

Jesus takes them to the Father. "Remember that woman at the well? This is for her, but not only her. There will be others, Father. Other women who have no hope, no future except humiliation and condemnation."

BAM! The nail rips through the tender flesh.

"And there were all those sick people. Some sick by their own doing, sick with sin and decay by their own choice, others ill with physical conditions for which there seems no healing."

BAM! The blood runs freely. Jesus willingly lays down His life for those who knew Him not and for those who were yet to be born—for all.

The influence of time on earth grew Jesus into a man of flesh and blood, emotion and memories. The influence of time on a cross sent Jesus back to heaven, back to the Father in loving intercession that will forever change our lives on earth.

How has time influenced your life?

3

Contingency Plans

Not long ago I was on an extensive driving trip and happened to be taking one of the bridges across Lake Pontchartrain. It wasn't that really long one that has you out there over the water wondering if you'll ever see dry land again, but it was several miles in length and made me anxious for shore nevertheless.

Now, on this day it was clear and bright and very beautiful. The water glistened and rippled gently in the breeze, and traffic was moving into the New Orleans area at a steady, unhurried pace. At least that was the case on our bridge. Our two lanes were just fine as we headed south, but the bridge beside us, carrying the northbound traffic, had come to a grinding halt.

You could see the traffic backed up for miles, while in the middle of this long-distance bridge, an accident was blocking both lanes. An ambulance was in attendance, as were law enforcement officers, and while they seemed to be completely focused on the accident at hand, hundreds of people behind them were suddenly at their mercy.

Most of the drivers had shut off their engines. Some were just sitting there looking tired, angry, and disgusted; some had gotten out of their vehicles and were engaged in conversation with other drivers. But one man in particular caught my attention. He was a handsome man, probably in his late twenties or early thirties. He wore dress pants and a long-sleeved white dress shirt with a tie. He had clearly just come from or was headed to his job or some other function that required his attire. He looked clearly out of place as he stood beside his car, a long pole in hand. He was fishing in Lake Pontchartrain from the railing of the bridge!

Because our traffic had slowed somewhat, I got a good look at this man. His face betrayed nothing but pure contentment. Here he was in rush-hour traffic, at a standstill because of someone else's carelessness, and he had found contentment.

I thought of the verse in Philippians 4:11, when Paul said, "I have learned to be content whatever the circumstances." I thought too of how impatient I would have been in the same situation. Stuck on a bridge in the heat of the afternoon, no hope in sight for a quick solution, no means of escape.

But this man, the very epitome of contentment, had something that made the difference for him. What was it?

He had a contingency plan.

Now, it may seem silly, but I found more value in this lesson than in a month of Sunday sermons preached from a pulpit. I saw by example what I knew God had in mind for me to learn and take to heart. Situations would arise in life—disappointments, heartaches, roadblocks. But if I had a contingency plan, my contentment need not be breached. My happiness would not be threatened by a mere inconvenience.

Did the man really want to fish off the Lake Pontchartrain bridge? I doubt it. I mean, I doubt that he had set out to go fishing that day. Oh sure, the pole had been stored in the back of his car. I could see the trunk lid was open. But the man was obviously not dressed for fishing. I doubt he left work that afternoon, thinking, "I sure hope something stops traffic on the lake bridge so I can get out and do some fishing."

Yet there he was.

Contingency plans are an important means to happiness in everyone's lives, but especially Christians. Jesus had such plans. He didn't impose himself on people, but rather dealt with things as they came along. People gathered for healing when He was on His way to rest; someone needed to be raised from the dead, and He stopped to heal someone else on the way; His mother told Him of the need for wine at the wedding feast, and even though it was not the time to reveal who He was, He told them to fill the pots with water, and they poured out wine. Rather than allow the unconventional to frustrate Him, Jesus allowed His plans to be altered without taking it as a personal affront or assault on His happiness.

How many times has something happened to alter your plans? It's happened to me a lot, and many times I take it quite personally. I might have had something figured out to the last possible second. I knew just what I wanted to accomplish and when, and I had all my ducks in a row, behaving rather nicely. Then suddenly, both lanes get blocked and I find myself on a bridge in the middle of a lake with traffic backed up in front and behind me, and my plans go down the drain. Sound familiar?

Maybe it has happened to you when you planned to be at work for a big meeting, and you discover you have a flat tire and no spare in the trunk. Maybe you found yourself unexpectedly pregnant after having put away diapers and bottles in exchange for weekend getaways now that your kids were grown. Maybe the doctor said, "I'm sorry, but your disease is terminal."

All your plans—good plans, productive plans—went suddenly by the wayside. Along with hope and joy and peace. A contingency plan would have been a breath of fresh air in the midst of your crisis, but you were fixed on your course, certain of your pre-arrangements. Nothing would interfere. Nothing could go wrong.

Maybe you did organize everything perfectly. Usually a roadblock has nothing to do with anything for which you have been responsible. It's out of your hands—out of your control. And if you're like me, that only makes it worse.

Contingency is defined by the *American Heritage Dictionary* as "a fortuitous or possible event." Things happen. Things we don't plan on; things that take place quite by accident. They don't come along asking our permission, but neither do they always seek our personal injury. The man fishing on the bridge proved that to me. He could have taken the whole matter very personally. He could have ranted and raved and shaken his fists, as others were doing. He could have pounded on the steering wheel or sounded his horn, as if either one would have made the cars suddenly start moving again. But instead, he had a plan. Obviously he had done this kind of thing before. At least it appeared that way. He seemed quite at ease with the situation.

The trunk of his car was open, and he didn't seem at all uptight about filling his time with an activity that didn't involve watching and waiting for his chance to get off the bridge and back to his original schedule. His contingency plan was perfect for the moment. He was content to let others deal with their problems— problems that had forestalled his original plans. While they worked out the situation, he had a course of action that allowed him to be at peace. After all, their problems were temporary, nothing permanent, and certainly nothing personal.

But contingency plans require something of us. First, we need to make ample provision for the unexpected.

The first provision is a change of attitude. Can we yield our right to having our ducks cemented in a row and accept that life happens, and that it isn't always a personal matter? That sometimes we come across someone else's roadblocks? Can we also see that even though someone else may interfere with our plans, even intentionally, we don't have to allow it to ruin our day? Can we also accept the fact that sometimes God brings about a change in our plans for our own good or the good of others? Jeremiah 29:11 says, " 'For I know the plans I have for you,' declares the Lord . . ." He has a plan for us, and sometimes our plan is very different from God's. Can we have an attitude of heart that says when our plans fall apart, just perhaps, God has interceded on our behalf to save us from something or guide us to something better?

Next, a contingency plan requires an optional viewpoint. When something causes our plans to change or come to a sudden halt, can we take up our "fishing pole" and wait it out until the interruption is cleared? Can we refuse to take it personally, and instead, choose another method of action until the way is made open for our original plan? Better yet, can we accept that our original plan might not have been the right plan?

It's hard sometimes to believe that God really knows what's going on. Harder still to imagine that He cares about whether we get to work on time, or that we get the perfect house we've been searching to buy, or that we find Mr. or Ms. Right to marry. But God does care, and when our plans go awry, we can bank on the fact that God has a contingency plan for us. It may not come in the shape of a fishing pole, but it's out there if you bother to search for it.

Think about the things that have happened to you today. Did you have any roadblocks? Did something stand in the way of what appeared to be the best path for you? Did life somehow give you lemons, but refuse to help you make lemonade? Next time, have a contingency plan. When things fall apart, try not to take it so seriously. Realize that the little old woman driving the huge sedan in front of you is not going five miles an hour to cause you grief. Recognize that the utility company's data entry clerk really hadn't considered your feelings when she accidentally keyed in the wrong account number that resulted in your electricity being turned off. Try not to feel that it's a personal attack when the ATM machine doesn't work or the grocery store has run out of your favorite brand.

Have a back-up plan. Have a hope—a change of heart—a peace about the things to come. Find the source of contentment that seems to elude folks now and again, and cling to it for all you're worth, for that source is Jesus, and the peace He offers is very real.

And to the man who chose to fish that day on Lake Pontchartrain: Thank you! Thank you for being a part of God's plan for me. Without realizing it, your peace in the midst of conflict helped me—taught me—influenced me. I don't know who you are or where you are now, but one thing I feel confident of: There's a fishing pole in the trunk of your car and the peace of contentment in your heart.

4

Charred Sticks and Stones That Roll

On a trip to Yellowstone National Park, I was amazed and overwhelmed at the beautiful landscape. The geysers were fascinating, the wild life amusing and a little frightening, and the people wonderfully animated.

But just when I thought I had the big picture in mind, God took me in a totally different direction, and the lesson He taught me there was most valuable. Amid the beauty of this national park were thousands of acres of fire-scarred land. The area was stark: a mournful reminder of tragedy.

Tall, blackened sticks rose out of the earth. Nothing grew on them. They were lifeless. The scene went on for miles and miles and left me feeling sad. Then to my surprise, I noticed other things: little flowers growing in between the blackened columns. Smaller, green trees, lush with life, struggling to rise from the ashes. The forest wasn't dead, but the overwhelming evidence of the tragedy that had struck so many years earlier was shadowing the truth. The worst that could happen to a forest had happened, and the scars were still there. But beyond that, growth and renewal were also evident, and it was here that I saw my life lesson.

Not so long ago I experienced a tragedy too. And like that mighty forest fire, the destruction swept through and destroyed the lush green growth that had been my life. When the fire died out, I felt there was little left but black stubs and vast, charred wastelands. I felt ugly and useless. Nothing seemed right, and though I refused to give up hope in God, I felt perhaps He might have been a tad overworked on the day that brought my blackest hour. Maybe He'd been a bit too busy to notice what had happened to one of His children.

It was easy to see the charred remainders. It's easy to see them now. What's not so easy to recognize is the growth that has come from the fire. The little things. The love of good friends and family. The unexpected help that nurtured me.

There are flowers growing, and saplings are striving to push up past the ashes. There is life amid death. Hope in the midst of adversity. But it's so much easier to see the dead trees.

I think of Mary and Martha and all the friends who'd gathered at the tomb when Lazarus died. Their grief was more than they could bear. Their hope had been that the tragedy would be averted. They had, after all, sent for Jesus. They knew He could keep this horrible thing from happening.

But He hadn't come. At least not in time. Death had marked their family—robbed them of their loved one and betrayed their hope. Now there was nothing but cold stone and black stubs. Desolation and death were all they could see. And even when Jesus showed up, all they could say was "If you'd only been here . . ."

They could see nothing but death and its finality. They didn't recognize the fact that Jesus causes life to sprout anew. They knew that they would all be together again someday. But right now that big stone across the tomb was more than they could contend with. It cancelled all other possibilities. It overwhelmed their hope.

I've always been impressed with the story of Lazarus. Not only for the obvious show of Jesus' ability to raise the dead; not even for the fact that Jesus wept. There was another aspect of this story that caught my attention. Before Jesus commands the dead, before He brings Lazarus back to life, He tells the people to take away the stone.

He could have supernaturally moved the rock himself. He could have raised His hands and blasted it into a million pieces. He could have caused Lazarus to walk right through it. But He didn't. Have you ever wondered why?

I think I know. At least I want to venture a guess.

I think many times in our lives we need resurrecting. We need to come out of the tomb and back from the dead. Sometimes we need it for ourselves, and sometimes we need it for someone we love. Either way, I believe we have to be willing to *remove the stone*. Sometimes we have to be willing to take out the black stubby pieces and cast them aside. To see beyond the burn. Sometimes we have to let go of the past and be willing to look to the new life of the future. Easy task? No way!

I think Jesus knew the people well enough to know that they would argue with Him. And, of course, they did. "He's gonna stink,

Lord. He's been in there four days now."

Then Jesus asks them, "Did I not tell you that if you believed, you would see the glory of God?" (John 11:40).

Do you know what they did next? They acted on faith they could only hope was valid. They took away the stone, and Jesus raised Lazarus from the dead. But as important as it is that Lazarus was resurrected, I think it is crucial that the people removed the stone first.

Maybe something bad has happened to you. The horror of it has left you defeated and overcome with grief. Maybe you're even saying to God, "If you'd only been here . . ."

The blackened fields stretch out around you; the charred stubs stand as lifeless reminders of what was once beautiful and fertile ground. Maybe your husband has announced he wants a divorce. He's found someone else. Could be that job you loved suddenly went up in flames. You find yourself laid off, let go in the wake of downsizing. Maybe your child has experimented one too many times with drugs, and now the police want you to identify her body at the morgue.

You stare out at the devastated land—the cold tomb. "If you'd only been here, God," you say. "If you'd only seen and cared enough to stop this before it got this far."

But He was there. And He is here, and He does care.

It's easy to see the negative, the horrible bits left behind. The scars are ugly and the eradication complete. But what He showed me in my own life is that I'm not alone, and that I have only to believe and to act on that belief. To take away the stone so that I might see the glory of God.

God is still in the business of resurrecting lives. It's not something we have to wait for until the end of time. He does it on a daily basis. He does it in ways that bring life out of the ashes of death.

That woman you know who lost her child and husband in a car accident. The man who can't seem to quit gambling. Those sad, lost souls who are only going through the motions of life but have no direction, no hope. He can bring them back to life. He can bring them out of the tomb.

But we have a responsibility. We must be willing to take away the stone. We must act on what we profess to believe. If we leave the stone in place, we won't see God at work. If we wrap ourselves up in the charred reminders of what might have been, of what once was, we might fail to see the new growth that springs up right beneath our feet.

What stones are you refusing to let go of? What stones are you refusing to move?

Think about the sorrow you've experienced, the hopelessness you've known. Do you need to be resurrected? I know just the one who can help.

Gather up your courage, put a little spit on your hands, and give a mighty shove. Move that stone. See beyond the fire and the charred remains of what might have been.

God's glory is just around the corner, and He wants to share it with you. He's in the business of bringing life out of death. Let us be in the business of moving stones.

5

My Daddy Is Good

I sat in the airport the other day waiting for a connecting flight home. I was tired, but the trip had been a real blessing, and so it was a good tired. The kind that comes from a sense of deep satisfaction.

As I sat there waiting, I found myself watching people once again. It was only moments before a uniformed flight attendant came up with a child in hand. The girl looked to be no more than nine or ten. She had lovely chocolate brown eyes, black hair, and the sweetest smile.

"Sit here," the attendant instructed. "I'll come and get you when it's time for the flight."

The girl nodded and took the seat beside mine.

"Don't worry, now," the attendant said with a smile. "I'll just be standing right over here. I'll be able to see you the entire time."

The girl nodded and began to swing her legs back and forth.

I smiled at the girl as well. I told her my name and broke the rule about talking to strangers. I figured she was safe. I told her I was heading home after being gone almost a week. I told her that I had a little boy her age. She waited politely for me to finish, all the while swinging her legs. She told me her name and then added that she was traveling from Texas to Missouri to see her sister.

I was so compelled by this girl's ease. She seemed completely content to be traveling alone. Perhaps she had done this numerous times, I thought. Perhaps this was an old routine that she'd grown up with. I decided to ask.

"Do you travel by yourself a lot?"

She shook her head and grinned an infectious grin that warmed my heart. "Nope, this is my first time."

I was impressed. "Are you afraid?" I asked, thinking that if she was, I could offer her some kind of encouragement or conversation until she was on her way once again. Little did I know that she would be the one to offer encouragement.

"Nope. I'm not afraid. My daddy told me things before I got on the airplane."

I was intrigued. What things had her father said that so easily put her at rest about this trip? I hated to pry, but I needed to know. I've been flying for a good part of my adult life, and I'm still not at ease as much as this child.

"So what did your daddy tell you?" I asked.

She gave a little bouncing momentum to her leg swinging. "He told me I didn't need to be afraid. He told me everything would be okay."

I nodded, trying to encourage her confidence, but she needed no encouraging. "He sounds like a very good daddy."

She nodded in rhythm to the bounce and swing. She was a body in perpetual motion. "He is a good daddy," she declared. "He loves me."

She said it with such confidence that I was thinking about her long after the attendant led her away for her next flight.

Her words reminded me of my heavenly Daddy. He too is a good daddy. The best of fathers. And He loves me. I couldn't help but think of the girl's confidence in this now distant man. He had told her she didn't need to be afraid, that everything would be okay.

Joshua 1:9 came to mind: "Have I not commanded you? Be strong and courageous. Do not be terrified; do not be discouraged, for the Lord your God will be with you wherever you go."

Our Daddy says we don't have to be afraid. We don't have to be terrified.

Is something scaring you? Are you trembling in fear, uncertain of the future? Maybe the bills are all due next week or even today, and there's no money in the bank to cover them. Maybe you've prayed and prayed for healing, but the tests keep indicating a problem.

Perhaps someone is threatening you—hovering nearby to cause you harm. Maybe someone wants to see you fired . . . evicted . . . divorced . . . dead. You're afraid to answer the door for fear of who might be on the other side.

"Be strong and courageous . . . do not be terrified."

Our Daddy is good. He loves us.

Do you believe that? Do you have the faith of a child who upon boarding a plane for a cross-country trip takes the words of her father to heart and has no fear? A child who fairly dances in her seat in anticipation of the journey ahead, even though she is making it alone for the first time?

"Do not be discouraged."

The problems of this world are temporary. Like dust in the wind—momentarily stirred up and then blown away. Our Father promises us that He will be with us wherever we go. He promises us that we don't have to make the journey alone.

Our Daddy is good. He loves us. Take it from the heart of a child who knows. Take it to heart and know for yourself. There will always be problems and conflicts. There will always be things that threaten our balance, our hope. But God is good. He's told us some things before we ever started the journey. He's given us words of wisdom—measures of advice—love letters in His Holy Word.

That little girl helped me to remember that faith is knowing who you're dealing with. She knew her daddy. Her nine or ten years of dealing with him gave her confidence in his behavior and credibility. When he told her it would be okay, she knew she could trust the matter to be right. She knew it because she trusted the one who spoke the words.

Do you trust the one who spoke the Word? Can you have the hope in your heavenly Father that this child had in her earthly one?

Listen. Our Daddy is speaking. He's telling us things . . . things we can take with us . . . things that will help us on our journey.

Are you listening?

Maybe you should take a seat for this one. Grab a copy of the Bible. Cross your legs at the ankle and start swinging them. Now give a little bounce.

Your Daddy loves you . . . and . . . He's got some things to tell you.

6

Fitting Into the Big Picture

My son is the self-proclaimed, undisputed Lego king of the world. He has loved those pesky building blocks since he was a tiny guy. Now, in case you've somehow missed out on those wonders of modern invention, let me tell you—someone was a genius. These colorful plastic building blocks are just what the doctor ordered for occupying young children.

They've made these blocks in every color known to man: some basic reds, blues, and whites—my son swears greens are harder and harder to find. Then there are the more spirited pinks for the girls and blacks and grays for your castle warriors and ninja fighters.

Square blocks aren't the only thing that come in the set. They have arches and long, thin rectangles. They have wheels and little Lego trees. They even have people.

Legos have been a main staple of this family for as long as my son has been old enough to walk and then some. There was even a time when my older daughters were into the building blocks, but that passed, giving way to fashion dolls and accessories. With my son, the Lego relationship goes on and on.

Now, I've watched my son build with these blocks. Sometimes he works from a kit with instructions, and sometimes he creates on his own. He has a vast Lego village in his bedroom—no need to go to the theme park, we have our own right here. Erik meticulously lays out the things he needs, working with his medium like a painter works with oils. There's a reason and a purpose for every piece, every move. He has hundreds of little pieces before him, but better yet, he has a picture in his mind of what it will all become.

And like my son with his toys, God has a picture of what our lives will become. We see hundreds of little pieces, but God already knows what the finished product will be, and it doesn't matter if He's working from His own set of instructions or just knows in His mind what He wants to accomplish—He has a plan.

Recall what Jeremiah 29:11 says: " 'For I know the plans I have for you,' declares the Lord."

Do you see those words? I mean, really see them? Are you listening to what they say?

"I know the plans I have for you."

God isn't just winging this. He didn't just wake up one day and say, "You know, maybe I should putter around with humankind this morning."

He has a plan.

He knows that plan.

That plan is for you.

Like my son with his universe of colorful plastic blocks, God has a universe of His own. This universe is His own creation, and we are the pieces that He works with. He looks down upon us, seeing all the possibilities, all the potential.

Erik knows the potential of his blocks. "You see this part over here?" he asks me. "Well, that's not really stable ground, so I have to put in a better support before I can build on it."

God knows the potential of His people. "You see this woman over here? Well, she's really not on stable ground. I'll have to put in better support before I can build on her."

My son looks to his creation with love. He has been known to cry when things fall apart or get angry when things won't work together.

God looks to His creation with love. He sees the homeless people, the abused and wounded children, the neglected and forgotten elderly. Do you suppose He cries when things fall apart for us? Do you suppose when He sees people refusing to work together to build a community, a church, or a home, that He gets angry because things aren't working together? I think He does. I think, like my son, God desires that His creation come together in perfect order. I think He desires the beauty and loveliness—the perfection of His kind of order.

I think that, like Erik, God sees the potential of a hundred million pieces and reaches out to set things in motion. He builds a foundation, strong and secure. He takes a willing heart and makes it into something useful, something beautiful.

"You have to put these pieces together first, Mom," my son tells me. "If you don't, the whole thing will fall apart later. And," he admonishes, "if you don't put the pieces in the right place, then the next row won't fit together right."

His message makes me smile, because unlike the Legos that have no choice of where their creator puts them, we have a choice of whether or not we go where God guides us, whether we stay on the firm foundation or head over to a less stable area of life.

We don't see the big picture. We don't understand that millions of pieces can come together in perfect order when given over to the master builder. We only see chaos and disorder. We see partially built creations and set about trying to hurry the process to completion. Never mind that we get pieces out of place or that the next row won't fit right. We'll build around it. We'll bridge over it. We'll find a way to go on, and rather than doing it right, we'll do it our way. Anything to show progress. Anything to be in charge.

I learned a saying many years ago and have always loved it. It has become my mantra, so to speak. It has definitely guided my days from time to time. What is this profound wisdom?

Have your ducks in a row.

As an organized person, I've not only got those ducks in a row, but they are also color-coded and numbered for easy reference. My ducks know where they go and where they don't go. They are perfectly ordered for maximum benefit.

A while back my ducks got out of line. They not only got out of the line but they also began to scatter all over the field. Some of the ducks didn't even bother to stick around, while new, trouble-making ducks decided to join the party.

I ran in a wild display of freakish ambition, trying to rearrange my ducks. I'd no sooner make a tiny bit of progress with the ducks nearest to me, when I'd have to turn my attention on those ducks about to be run over by the express trains of life. By the time I turned back to the few ducks I'd managed to reorganize—well, you can imagine what had happened. That's right, they were off and running again.

My Lego pieces were scattered—my ducks were running amuck—life just plain didn't make sense, and I couldn't begin to conceive that God had a plan for me. Much less that I could follow it up with the next portion of that verse: "plans to prosper you and not to harm you."

Whoa! Hold it right there. I can tell you here and now, I didn't feel prospered. I felt harmed. Run over. Smashed upon the rocks. Devastated.

Ever feel that way? Have you ever felt like God was standing over you with a God-sized flyswatter, ready to do business? Boy, I did.

I tried to rationalize it, telling myself, "Perhaps God is bringing you new ducks. Perhaps He doesn't like the ducks you're working with now."

I tried to get all pious and religious. Sanctification and spiritualization required the contemplation of the ramifications. Huh? Those ducks were speaking a foreign language.

I tried to blame myself. *Maybe if I'd only nailed those little duck feet to the floor . . . Maybe if I'd caught the very first duck to move . . .*

I tried to blame others. "Okay, who moved my ducks?"

I tried to dance around the issues at hand. *Maybe these aren't really my ducks. Maybe I'm in the wrong place and these are somebody else's ducks.*

But over and over God kept bringing me back to Jeremiah 29:11: "plans to give you hope and a future."

Let me tell you, when my world is in disorder, I have very little hope. When I look at that pile of Legos or the ducks running amuck, I feel completely hopeless. What possible order can come from this disorder? How can things ever be right again?

Maybe you've been there too. Maybe God started you out on a good foundation: all the pieces fit. But then you moved your pieces, or, worse yet, had them moved for you, and now the foundation isn't quite so solid.

I remember a Christian family in our community: a pastor, his wife, and their two children; a wonderful family, who expressed true Christian love to their neighbors, their church, and their town. Their foundation was solid—their ducks were in a row. Then a man who had slipped through the justice system murdered their daughter. Their ducks scattered: the murderer moved their pieces.

The beautiful creation that had started out as a lovely family not only lost pieces of their structure . . . they lost a beautiful child who had given them many moments of love and hope. A child who had shared the Gospel with her friends. A child who did not deserve the early fate she got.

This event totally shook me. After all, here was a family who served the Lord in fervent love and joy. This girl's mother must have prayed for her children as I did mine. This girl's father surely worked to see his family spiritually fed and growing in the truth.

I couldn't see the big picture. I couldn't look at the pile of colored blocks and broken dreams and see how God could possibly make anything good out of this chaos. I felt afraid. I argued with God.

"You had the power, Lord, to keep this horrible thing from happening, so why didn't you?"

I mourned this child's passing as if I knew her personally. I thought of the waste—the utter and complete waste. I thought of justice and revenge. I thought of how unfair it was, how it might have been one of my daughters.

Then I became scared.

"Plans to give you hope and a future."

Those words seemed so distant. So difficult.

But then something amazing started to happen. Like wildfire, the word began to spread. One person after another was touched by this child's life as much as they were by her death. School friends began to talk of her faith in Jesus Christ. Kids who had only heard of this child began seeking salvation and a way out of the mire that had become their existence.

God was building with His blocks. Here a red one. There a blue. Oh, and don't forget those hard-to-find green ones.

Adults hardened by the difficulties of life wept openly at the poetry penned by this child. They listened to the stories told of her faithfulness, of her witness. They watched the family who chose to focus on their love and the joy of their child rather than on the man who stole her from them.

God knew the bigger picture. He knew what was to come down the road. What seemed chaotic and hopeless to us was but a flashing moment to Him.

"I know the plans I have for you . . . plans to prosper and not to harm. . . ."

He's in control. He sees beyond the hopelessness. He is lighting up the darkness and settling down to work. To once again make order out of disorder, to gather His loved ones together.

Maybe lost children instead of ducks.

Maybe hearts instead of building blocks.

The light falls across His workbench in the shape of a cross . . . the shape of hope and a future.

7

The Waiting Is the Hardest Part

Waiting has never been my forte. Just ask anyone who knows me. I don't wait in ease. Those verses that speak to letting the Lord fight the battle, while I sit still, are ones I figured He wrote for someone else. Resting in the Lord, hiding in the shelter of His protection, waiting for Him to act, those seem to be situations of inactivity, and I'm a very active person.

My oldest daughter reminds me of myself in that way. She wants quick resolution and instantaneous results. Sometimes it doesn't even have to be the best result, just any result. Anything at all that implies life is moving forward.

To say I live life in the fast lane wouldn't exactly be accurate. I'm not jet-setting and running from party to party. Neither am I given over to hundreds of great causes and entertainments. But if life in the fast lane means that I seldom sit still long enough to catch my breath—nor can anyone around me—then I'm guilty as charged.

There's just something about waiting that irritates me. I can't stand to be put on hold, and yet time and time again I find it seems to be my lot in life. I called the phone company the other day, and after making nearly a dozen choices of pressing either #1 or #2, I was finally connected to a computerized voice that told me all the customer assistants were busy at that moment, and would I please hold for the next available assistant?

Waiting is like being told, "You aren't important enough to deal with just yet." Waiting is like being the last kid picked for the baseball team. Waiting is—well, it's hard.

It shouldn't be hard. After all, there's really nothing you have to *do*. You have to wait, but what is that?

I figure waiting is like that moment at your senior prom when the music ends. You're out there on the dance floor, uncertain whether you'll dance the next dance or sit down. You want to wait for the next song to start, but you don't want to look stupid standing there. Waiting is a passage of time over which I have no control. And that's what grieves me—the loss of control.

I've been a control freak all my life. I just want to do things my way. I've always prided myself in being a person of action. A person who gets things done. I've always wanted people to know they could count on me; that when they had a need, I was able to jump in and supply the solution. Because besides being a control freak, I'm also a fixer.

And that brings us back to the issue of waiting. Fixers hate to wait around. Waiting doesn't get things fixed. Fixing requires immediate action. It requires wheels to be turning and buttons to be pushed, and it requires that the fixer have a planned course of action. After all, we fixers have a lot to fix.

So having bared my soul and explained my faults (at least a few of them), I have to admit that one of the most important lessons God has had to teach me deals with waiting. It hasn't been pleasant, and often it's been pretty ugly.

But sometimes we have to wait. Sometimes we have to let go of controlling and fixing. Sometimes my way isn't the high way—the way of God.

Isaiah 30 is a chapter that deals rather strongly with those of us who struggle with waiting on the Lord. Right from the start of this chapter, I found myself faced with an admonition. "Woe to the obstinate children," declares the Lord, "to those who carry out plans that are not mine."

Hmmm. I thought I was carrying out plans that I'd cleared with God. I mean, I had that thirty-second prayer on the way to the grocery store, and I didn't see any signs that said NO. Of course, there was that sign that said STOP, but I figured that wasn't from God.

The verse in Isaiah goes on: "forming an alliance, but not by my Spirit, heaping sin upon sin; who go down to Egypt [you can fill in just about any destination here] without consulting me."

How many of us are guilty of that one? Did I see a few hands raised? A few twitching smiles? Go ahead, admit it—it's just between you and God, after all. And He already knows all about it.

The chapter tells further how those obstinate children sought help in all sorts of different places. They looked to fix things in one way or another, and all of it was utterly useless. God called them rebellious, deceitful, unwilling to listen to His instruction. He promises there will be destruction because of their sin. And then God slips in a verse that left me feeling close to tears.

Verse 15 says, "This is what the Sovereign Lord, the Holy One of Israel, says: 'In repentance and rest is your salvation, in quietness and trust is your strength, but you would have none of it.'"

I have to admit, I saw myself in this chapter. Rushing about, seeking help here and there, refusing to wait for God's hand—always having to have some portion of control. How it must have grieved Him. The Sovereign Lord, the Holy One of Israel, the Father who had promised faithfulness to a faithless generation. But they didn't want to wait for that. We often don't want to wait for it either.

What if God is too late? What if this time when we're backed up against the Red Sea, God fails to show up in time to part the water, and we are captured by the Egyptians? (Those folks we thought at one time might be helpful to us, and instead they enslaved us.)

What if God is taking a break? What if He's put the answering machine on and isn't taking His calls? Sound silly? Maybe so, but I know I've had those worries before. Worries that said, "I got myself into this mess, after all. It isn't God's fault, so therefore I should get myself out of it." Or better yet, how about that old adage "God helps those who help themselves?"

We want a fast-food God, a one-hour photo God. A God who works instantaneous results with no waiting. A God who offers an express lane to conflict resolution and self-gratification.

But waiting is often something we're called upon to do, and we must begin to see this. God has a purpose and a plan even in those quiet, seemingly barren moments of rest. He has the control, and that is what we must give over to Him in order to see our needs met. Sometimes that comes easy, and sometimes it doesn't, but it will be required of all of us sooner or later.

Maybe we need to practice waiting. After all, if something is foreign to you, you only learn it by practice. If you want to play the piano, you must practice. If you want to speak a foreign language, you need to practice it. And I'm pretty sure that if you want to learn to wait, you must practice waiting.

"Take five," God says. "Sit a spell. Here, I have a nice comfy spot right under my wing."

Did I see some shoulders slump? Somebody out there willing to admit they're tired and just plain worn out?

Don't be one of God's stiff-necked children—the obstinate, who would have nothing to do with repentance, rest, quietness, and trust. Pull up a chair—better yet, crawl up on God's lap and rest in arms that care. Hey, it's practice time!

8

I See Dead People

This catchy little phrase, popularized by a recent Hollywood movie, is one I've heard repeated in all kinds of settings. Lately it's been driven home to me in one particular area of my life. One that came as quite a shock.

My father-in-law, Fred, a big, husky guy who always managed to get more done in a day than most folks managed in a week, was stricken with cancer. The prognosis wasn't good. The cancer was stage four, the worst, and he needed immediate surgery. The hope of the doctor was to buy time for Fred. The hope of the family was for a full cure.

In the process of dealing with this, I became one of the drivers to take Fred back and forth to the doctors and hospitals for his various treatments. At first, this was rather disturbing. I saw this once healthy man dwindling before my eyes, and I saw the other folks who frequented those radiation and chemotherapy stations.

People in various stages of cancer. People in various stages of dying.

I saw dead people.

People who were there one week and gone the next. People who had fought the good fight as best they could only to reach the point in battle where the enemy defeated them. Old people. Young people. Death has no respect for age.

When you hang out in radiation treatment waiting rooms, you have a tendency to get to know the other patients. You pick up the lingo and speak like a pharmacist as you share what the doctors are trying in order to kill the cancer. You exchange the names of companies who carry merchandise that will help ease the miseries of the disease. You cling to each other, because you know the score better than those on the outside of this tight little world. Even so, I was the odd man out in a very selective club. I was healthy.

After a time, though, I got to know folks a little better. I learned that Helen's last day of radiation would be Friday and that she and her husband were going out to celebrate. I listened to John talk about his recurring cancer and his hope that chemotherapy combined with radiation would bring him back into remission so that he could go fishing with his grandkids. I learned that Julie was a fighter extraordinaire, and that she'd been battling cancer off and on for three years. She had a raw, cynical edge to her, but at the same time she was one of the funniest, brightest points to our day.

If the doctor was late, Julie would call out, "Hey, I know more about that machine than he does anyway. Let me have a go at it. How about it, Fred? You want me to run the machine today?"

She gave us laughter in the face of horror. She made the situation bearable, because she reminded us that we were not alone.

In return, the members of the group asked me about my father-in-law and how his treatment was coming along. We laughed and joked about everyday things, then laughed and joked about bald heads, selective sunburns from localized radiation, and other insider-type issues.

For all of their problems, I'd never met a more alive group of people. These were seriously ill folks. Folks whose doctors, in many cases, didn't hold out much hope for recovery or cure, but who offered instead . . . time.

Precious time.

While watching these people interact and listening to their stories and words of encouragement for one another, I couldn't help but think that a good many of them would be gone in another few weeks or maybe years. They talked openly about time limits and the progression of their illness. They weren't morbid, but rather recognized their disease for the power that it had over frail human flesh.

"I'm dying to be done with chemotherapy," Julie told me, then laughed as though she'd just told the funniest joke in the world. The others laughed too. They knew and accepted that there were limitations to life, but they'd made choices to spend their final days living, instead of dying.

I see dead people.

Not just in radiation and chemotherapy waiting rooms. I see them in congregations—pew warmers who come week after week to religious services. They go through the motions of religion, but never accept what Jesus has to offer. They are always hearing but never understanding, seeing but never perceiving, as is spoken of in the sixth chapter of Isaiah.

The difference, however, is that those with cancer recognize their condition. But many of those in spiritual limbo haven't a clue. They don't understand their disease. They don't realize their need for treatment. Their cancer is spreading, eating them up from the inside out.

They come and go, and quite often can't remember what was said ten minutes after walking out the front door of the church. They close their Bibles at noon on Sunday and don't pick them up again until eleven o'clock the following Sunday. They are a burdened people. A busy people. A dying people.

Sometimes they listen quite well. They stake themselves out and go through all the motions and traditions. They can quote chapter and verse, but are still without understanding.

Often they see. They see the business end of the church. They see the numbers issues and the budgetary needs. They even see the problems related to giving themselves in service to the church. They are ever seeing, but never perceiving.

I see dead people.

People who are alone inside the emptiness of their souls. People who find no hope in the routine—no treatment for what ails them. They are a rather assorted collection of do-gooders and image gurus. People who point to their attendance like a badge of nobility, hoping that somehow occupying the third seat on the left-hand side of the fourth aisle will recommend them to the Father in heaven. People who are content to be dead, because they've never known life. Life in Jesus Christ.

Are you among the walking dead?

Are you just going through the motions, ever hearing but never understanding? Seeing, but never perceiving?

Do you want to hear?

Do you want to understand?

The hope that we have is a very real one. It's cause for celebration. The hope we have to cure our disease of sin is a one-on-one relationship with Jesus Christ.

Maybe you feel caught up in traditions. You go to church on Sunday and shake hands with all the right people. You smile and nod when you're supposed to and maybe even murmur a hesitant "amen" when the time is right. You recognize that there might be a problem, but you haven't a clue what the right treatment might be.

You want desperately to feel alive, but instead you are the walking dead.

Don't give up. Don't buy your grave plot just yet.

There's a treatment for this disease. The doctor is in.

Jesus offers himself in a real and very present way. He's the physician extraordinaire. He's the prescription and procedure for eliminating what ails you. He's the only cure your spirit will ever need.

Scared?

Afraid to diagnose that disease? Terrified to hear the words, "It's terminal"?

Jesus understands. He is the Great Physician, and the treatment for your need is as simple as letting go of your indifference and worries. It's as easy as releasing yourself to His care.

Dare to believe in the cure! Dare to believe that He has victory over death!

Let Jesus bring you to life. Celebrate what He has already done for you—what He offers as a free gift for the taking. His healing is complete, and He wants you to be whole. The cure is much better than the disease.

Oh, and if you think about it, celebrate on Friday night too. Helen's cancer is in remission, and she's looking for this to be a complete cure. I know if her determination and positive spirit have anything to say about it, we won't be seeing her again. She'll be too busy with living, and I think we should join her.

The Doctor is in. He's calling your name.

What will your answer be?

9

Dead-Heading in the Garden of Life

I 've tried over the years to develop my green thumb. I figured that with my grandmother and mother so heavily into gardening, I must have it in my blood. As a child, I didn't really see it as an important aspect of living. All that dirt and hard work seemed to tip the scales against the favorable outcome of flowers and vegetables. Now, if we could have grown chocolate in Kansas, I'm sure I would have been the first one in the garden every morning. But broccoli and cabbage just didn't have the same appeal.

As a teenager, I certainly didn't want to spend time sweating it out in a garden while all manner of creepy crawly things landed on me for an afternoon snack. I saw nothing productive or important about gardening even with my grandmother offering me bits of sage advice.

"It's important to keep your garden rows straight," she once told me. "You have to have something to measure against. A mark on which to hold yourself true. The same is true for Christians. Christians have a tough row to hoe. It's important that they keep their eye on the mark."

I thought her sweet and a bit silly in the analogy. She showed me how to take a stick and stake it out at the very edge of the garden, tie a string to it, then put another stake at the end of the row at the opposite edge. I dragged many a hoe under that string, with Grandma telling me to keep to the mark. She probably had the straightest rows in all of Topeka, maybe even all of Kansas.

Then there was my mother. She taught me about weeds. She told me her father had his own theory on weeds and passed it along to his children. "If something grows up where it's not supposed to be," he declared, "it's a weed." Recognizing weeds from the good plants was always one of my downfalls until my mother reminded me of the even rows. "See how you have that neat little row of growing plants and then you have those little green shoots that come up at the sides? Those are the weeds. They don't belong. They don't fit in the line."

I hated weeding, so I really didn't care who stayed in line and who didn't, but when I became an adult, I started to remember those little bits of wisdom. Gardening was suddenly more interesting for pleasure than for need. I didn't want to plant in order to can one hundred quarts of anything, like my grandmother used to do each season. I didn't even want to plant in order to have home-grown, fresh vegetables versus canned, store-bought ones. No, I wanted to plant for therapy, and I wanted to plant flowers for the beauty they offered.

Now, both my grandmother and mother planted vegetables as

well as flowers, and the same wisdom and advice followed for each.

"Plant in a specific order, and when things show up out of order, you'll know they don't belong there."

"Don't forget to water and feed those little plants. They can't get up and go to the kitchen for what they need."

When I started reading up on gardening, I added other bits of knowledge. Things I'd seen in practice but didn't remember hearing anything about in conversation. Things like working up the soil around a plant or mulching it or staking the plant. But perhaps one of the most fascinating things I read about was dead-heading.

What a term! My garden book states that you should dead-head any old blossoms at first sign of decay. Cut 'em out! Pop 'em off! Just get rid of those dead flower heads. I read on and was advised that by doing this, I would stop the flow of nutrients to blossoms that were no longer living, and thus the new buds would receive the extra food and water that might have gone to a blossom that was dead.

So out I went, snipping and clipping until I felt the garden had received an adequate haircut. I felt horrible about it. I mean, the blossoms were dead, true enough, but it seemed almost cruel to just step in there and muster them out. They'd been useful to me only days before. Their beauty and rich colors had given me a sort of energy for my day. Their sweet aroma, now turned rather putrid with decay, had been a delightful sensation to my nose.

The emotions of life are much the same. There is a time for anger to drive us forward into action. The Bible says, "Be angry, but sin not." It's not a sin to have anger—it's what you do with the anger that can create sin. I get angry at the injustice of abortion and euthanasia, but I would be sinning if I took that anger into the realm of killing the doctors who perform such deeds. I get angry when people vandalize my property, but again, I would be sinning if I returned the favor and vandalized theirs.

Anger is like a blossom that comes up in our life. Yes, it really is. It comes to flower in the heat of the moment or over a long period of development. Just like flowers. Anger really can be a good thing. Anger at the injustices of the world can drive us into service. Anger at ignorance can push us toward education. Anger at circumstances can often bring about a positive and beneficial change.

But if anger remains and isn't dead-headed after it serves its initial purpose, it begins to decay and turn ugly. That's when bitterness and rage take over. Their putrid smells and brown, dry petals do nothing to fuel the good, but do everything to drain the rest of the plant from the life-giving nutrients it needs to survive.

I knew a woman who vowed she would never forgive her father for the injustice of physical abuse. Beaten as a child by this demanding monster, she ran away as a teenager and found herself abused in many other ways. Her anger drove her, fed her, and eventually robbed her of a decent life. Daily she focused on her hatred and her bitter heart. She became undesirable in the eyes of her friends and family. No one wanted to deal with the decay and stench of her dying soul. She needed desperately to dead-head her anger, to let the other possibilities in her life have the rich nutrients that anger had robbed from them. The only trouble was, she hadn't a clue how to garden.

Enter the gardener. Jesus' identity was mistaken by Mary at the tomb. She thought he was the gardener, until He opened her eyes to see Him for who He really was. And in a very real way, He is our gardener. Jesus alone comes in, and if we allow Him, He cultivates, prunes, feeds, waters, and even dead-heads the garden of our lives.

Think of someone you know who when problems come reacts in such a manner that shows the gardener at work. Perhaps he is wrongly accused. Anger seeps in at the injustice of it all. Then he is proven to be guiltless, and the matter is cleared. The choices are rather well defined. Either the anger continues to dominate that person, robbing him of important energy and fuel, or anger is dead-headed, clipped out, and allowed to die.

Maybe anger isn't the blossom that needs to be pruned. Maybe desire has blossomed in your garden. Maybe you desire the same type of success your co-workers enjoy in their positions. They continue to move up the ladder, while you remain on the bottom rung. Never mind how they are advancing up that ladder, be it good or bad. You only see the possibilities that continue to pass you by. Desire gives way to envy and the blossom begins to wither.

Desire can be a good thing. Finding a goal and setting a dream into motion are positive ambitions that God honors. The Bible is full of examples of people who dreamed big, and God blessed them. Envy, however, is not something your Father wants for you. Envy is destructive. Envy is a dying blossom that is robbing you of the water and food you need for other blossoms.

But just as my flowers can't dead-head themselves, neither can we dead-head our blossoms turned bad. The Gardener must come and clip away the bad so that the good might live.

How's your garden today? Are you blooming with lively colors and fresh new buds that promise the loveliness and beauty you crave? Or are you full of dead flowers that need to be cut out? Maybe you aren't even aware of the way those old blossoms are stealing the potential for new growth. Maybe you've been wondering why your spiritual life is going nowhere: no growth, no beauty of Christ. My guess is that you need some dead-heading.

Jesus is ready to help. He's standing by with the shears. He knows exactly which are the good blooms and which are weeds. He knows what is dead and dying, and what is robbing you of your joy and strength. Don't be afraid to let him tend the garden of your life. He's a loving Master Gardener. He grew you this far, trust Him to grow you the rest of the way.

Angry because of false accusation?

Clip.

Feeling vengeful because of a family member's injustice?

Clip.

Turning Jesus loose to work in your garden can only be beneficial. Do you feel it? Do you feel the love and peace flowing up as the decay is trimmed away? Ah, you have a new bloom—you're showing new life! The Master Gardener is at work. He's pruning you, dead-heading the bad and nurturing the good. Here comes the living water!

"Grow, little ones!" he calls out. "Grow!"

10

Faith in the Light

The other day as darkness set in and the skies passed from a turquoise blue into that lovely shade of midnight navy, I sat staring at the light switch. There was still enough light to see the switch—the room was gray and shady, but not yet pitch black. I wondered. . . . Would the light come on when I flipped the switch?

Maybe it wouldn't. I only assumed it would. After all, I know nothing about what makes a light switch work. It stands to reason that I really should know how it all comes together in order to access it. I mean, are there wires that connect to thingamabobs? Are there little creatures who run along some magical line to bring that all-inspiring electricity to my lamp? How was it created?

If I don't know how it works, will it still work?

Silly as this may sound, we often deal with faith in God in the same manner. Darkness sets in, and we need light, but we're afraid to go to the source. What if God isn't there? What if He doesn't respond this time? After all, I don't know how God works or why. I wasn't there when He laid the foundations of the earth. I haven't a clue if He sends tiny messengers along some divine prayer line to bring power to my life.

I've heard so many arguments about faith. How can you believe in something you can't see? How can you believe that God will really work? How can you believe there is a God out there—that He listens, that He cares?

Now, I could give you all sorts of flowery statements. Things like "I can't see the wind, but I see the effects of the wind." But in Kansas, I have seen the wind. It's pretty visible. Some say Kansas means "people of the south wind." Others joke that the only reason we have any soil at all is because it blew up from Oklahoma. Then there are those mighty F-scale tornadoes. Wind in all its ugly glory. I've seen the wind, so that analogy to faith isn't the all-in-all for me.

I could say, "Well, look to the Bible for examples of faith." Moses had faith. I would too if I heard God talking to me from a burning bush or if He led me with a pillar of fire. I always found it hard to understand why people around Jesus had such a hard time seeing Him. I'm sorry, but you raise somebody from the dead, and I'm going to be pretty persuaded that you have something unique and special going on.

But even so, I suppose for me, rather than answer the questions "How can I believe that God will really work?" or "How can I believe God is out there?" I have to ask, "What's the alternative?"

If I fail to believe that God is who He says He is, that He will do what He says He will do, then what are my other choices? That

I'm my own God? That there is no God?

I suppose we could put our faith in money; after all, it's tangible. We can see money, and we definitely know the effect it has on the world. Money talks, and people listen. But tangible doesn't last; money loses its value as economies bounce up and down. What's here today is often gone tomorrow with a single plunge of the stock market. I often remember the story of a post-Civil War widow whose husband had buried a trunk full of Confederate money for them to use after the war. She ended up papering the walls with the valueless stuff.

Along with money, we could put our faith in things. Big houses and nice cars, pantries full of food, and closets full of clothes. Or we could put our faith in jobs and careers. We could pour ourselves into being and doing until we drop one day from the exhaustion of it all.

Maybe we should put our faith in people. We can see people. We can talk to people, and they talk back in very audible ways. We can ask people advice and direction, and they will no doubt give their opinions and suggestions. But people fail. People are fallible. They are often misinformed or influenced by the wrong things. They are sometimes motivated by personal need and serve ulterior motives.

So what's the alternative to putting our faith in God?

I think of the disciples and the daily walk they had with Jesus. As they went about their business, Jesus performed miracles and talked of the days to come. He healed the sick and raised the dead. He made banquets out of loaves and fishes, and He cast out demons. The disciples must have been amazed at Jesus' performance. The people who were around Jesus must have been in awe. How could they not believe? How could they not have faith in Jesus as Messiah after He called Lazarus out of the grave?

But their faith was weak, even nonexistent at times. After all, no one was sitting outside the tomb on the third day. No one expected to see Jesus again. If they'd had faith that He was who He said He was—if they'd had faith in what He said He would do, they would have been standing there waiting for Jesus to emerge from the tomb. Banners waving, new clothes for the King, a feast to celebrate.

Wouldn't you?

Should it have been any different than you or I dropping off a friend at the airport and being told, "I'll be back in three days"? Would you come back to pick up your friend or would you go hide and fret that he was gone and never coming home again?

Their faith was weak. Our faith is weak too. We stand at the light switch of prayer, wondering, "Will He really hear me?" "Will He really care?" "Is God really there?"

We fret and fuss. We hide away. And we are lost in much ado about nothing—the nothing being our absent faith.

Can you come up with an alternative to trusting in God?

Can you come up with a plan that successfully skirts the need to have faith in Jesus Christ as God's only Son, who died to bring us into right relationship with the Father?

I can't. I can't find it by putting my faith in money or time or people or things. I can't write it off as being unimportant, because frankly, the only thing that gets me through the day is believing that God is who He says He is.

Oh sure, sometimes I stand at the light switch and turn it on and off over and over, just to make sure God is still there. I see the coming darkness, and I run for the lamp. I sit in the brightness of day and leave the light on—just in case. I bask in the overwhelming hope that if I stay close to the Source of light, I'll never be in darkness again.

Faith isn't all that tricky. It isn't risky unless you consider giving up worry a risk. What's risky, in my estimation, is having no faith at all. Sitting in the darkness because you're sure the light won't come on—that this is somehow your lot in life. Cursing the darkness because you don't feel you have the right to go to the Source of light. Crying in the darkness, believing you're all alone, that light doesn't exist—at least not for you.

But the Light is there for you!

Faith is a confidence that the light is going to come on. Faith is daring to believe God is God and that He wants to light your way, that He hears you when you call, no matter how many times you flick the switch.

Because, believe it or not, God doesn't want to leave you in the dark. He loves you and wants to shine the light of His glory around you, on you, through you.

"Arise, shine, for your light has come, and the glory of the Lord rises upon you," says Isaiah (60:1). Have faith that these words are true. It doesn't take big faith, just little baby faith—faith that once put into practice will grow and grow and grow. It's up to you. Look at that verse again. There is action required of you.

Arise.

11

Bare Bones

I found myself at an event called a "Bare Bones Viewing." A society of historians had purchased the home of a famous fellow, and it was their intention to set the house back to its original order. The bare bones event was scheduled to earn money and to bring in local interest, and it did just that.

The house was a stately affair from the outside, but as you drew closer you could see the wear and tear of a century. Multiple coats of paint weren't wearing well, and the use and abuse of multiple owners had taken a big toll.

Inside, the house was in a state of disrepair. They were in the process of tearing down walls and ceilings. As I wandered through the gracious old lady with all her scars and modern additions, I thought of us as children of the ages. We were just like that old house.

The world has added a wall here or there to our hearts.

Philosophies and problems have brought down the ceiling and closed off unneeded bays and cubbyholes. Sorrow has chipped away at our paint and cracked our windows.

I think of the woman who cried her tears on Jesus' feet. Or the woman at the well whose life Jesus knew all about. Or even the adulterous woman who stood ready to be stoned, until Jesus' mercy stepped in.

Time had not been kind to these ladies. They bore the wear and tear of the ages, of a society who no longer valued them. Oh, they had started out pristine and lovely. There was great potential for their future. So what happened?

What always happens? Life got in the way.

Without warning, the paint began to chip away, and the pipes began to rust. The stairway railing was broken when someone ignorantly crashed against it. Someone carelessly broke a window or a heart, and never worried about its repair.

Maybe you know someone like that now. I do. I know many people who are in this state of disrepair, but one young woman stands out in my mind more than the others. She's worn and tired. She's mother to four children all under the age of eight. She's alone in the world, her husband having left her for another woman. Daily I see her go through her paces, a bit frayed at the edges, her structure suffering from time and abuse, her interior broken and rendered in pieces.

She must have been quite pretty in her youth, which hasn't been that long ago in days or years, but in experience she has reached beyond decades. She's one of the forgotten ones. One of the many who is merely struggling to exist, to survive the onslaught of time and the people who will come and go in her life. She isn't really living—she's enduring.

Like that old house. No one cared for it, at least not in a way that honored its original purpose: to be a home. It had been offices to government officials and for other businesses. It had even been lived in by other people, people who really didn't value it for the place it had once been.

The same was true for this young woman, and for those women I mentioned from the Bible. They were all used by other people for other purposes. They weren't valued for their original existence. God had created them for one reason, but life used them for another.

But the story doesn't end here. The bare bones viewing was designed to show the "before" condition in order to better appreciate the "after." Because the people who bought this house have every intention of restoring it to its original grandeur and beauty. The people who redeemed this structure from the broken-down office building that it had become have great plans for its future.

Jesus had great plans for those women in the Bible. He saw the bare bones. He saw the tragedy of careless years—the abuse of a society that had forgotten the value of human life. Jesus has great plans for the woman who lives in my neighborhood, and He has great plans for you.

Maybe you're the broken one. Maybe you've been used by a cruel world whose intentions were never to honor your original purpose. Maybe you feel hopelessly torn apart. Maybe the debris is stacked too high for any hope that someone can clear it all away and restore order.

Perhaps you know someone who has been ravaged and devastated by life. Someone who has fallen into a rut or a pit of despair. Someone who doesn't have the strength to get back up—or the heart to care anymore.

What if we as individuals or churches or neighborhoods started creating our own societies of restoration? What if we saw these broken-down people and brought them to the only one who can redeem them? The only one who can restore them to their original beauty and purpose?

The second chapter of Mark talks about the man who was lowered to Jesus on a mat. He had no way to bring himself before the Lord, so his friends did the job for him. Couldn't we do that for each other? Couldn't we reach outside our comfort zone just a little to care about the broken people in our lives?

Oh, I know what you might be thinking: *They've brought this on themselves. They'll just get down again. A person has to care about herself first before she can get help. What if they just turn around and dig themselves back into the same hole?*

Jesus didn't ask the man on the mat if he was crippled by his own hand. He didn't ask the man if he would go on to be a productive citizen. When the woman cried on Jesus' feet and dried her tears with her hair, He didn't suggest that while she was forgiven, she would have to show Him a clean record for a year before she could be blessed by Him.

Why do we worry so much about whether or not a hurting, damaged soul "deserves" our help, rather than simply offer the help?

Aren't you glad God doesn't have a roster of requirements for us to meet before He's willing to deal with us? Oh sure, we have to repent of our sins and ask for forgiveness in order to be forgiven, but I have yet to see examples of God refusing to welcome home the prodigal. Jesus did imply that whatever we do for the least of these, we do for Him.

It wasn't just a catch phrase or a bit of propaganda. Jesus was showing us the very heart and nature of who He was—who He is, and who He wants us to be.

You know, under the grubby, well-worn carpet at that house, soon to be a museum, I was told they found a beautiful hardwood floor. There are great plans to strip away the old carpet and polish the wood. There is potential for this house that many people have overlooked.

There is potential for the broken, tragic strangers in our lives. The strangers many people overlook.

Why not open your eyes to the possibilities and get out a mat? Grab a friend, maybe two, and help a soul in need to find the healing that Jesus offers. You just might find a beautiful heart underneath that grubby, well-worn façade. You just might offer hope to a dying soul that the world has long ignored.

Whatever you do for the least of these . . .

12

Is Your Christianity Showing?

I think the saddest and worst thing anyone ever said to me was "Oh, I didn't know you were a Christian." I remember the moment like it was yesterday. I was eighteen and newly employed for a national company. I felt very grown up and very important. This was a real job, with a real paycheck and even a parking place. I thought I had landed on top.

After being there for two or three weeks, we were all gathered in the break area discussing our weekend. One lady had gone boating and sported a new tan. Another had taken her children to the zoo. When it came my turn to speak, I just shrugged and said, "Oh, I didn't do much. I went to church yesterday, but that was about it." That was when one of my co-workers turned to me with sincere surprise and said, "Oh, I didn't know you were a Christian."

At the time, I didn't think a lot about it. I passed it off with some trivial talk about how I'd gone to church most of my life and that I had accepted Christ at an early age. Nothing much more was said, because our time was up, and we all headed back to our cubicles. But not long after that, I began to feel a nagging in my spirit.

Why didn't she know I was a Christian?

Had I acted in some way that would suggest otherwise? Had I been unkind or uncivil to those around me? Had I dressed or talked in a manner that would show me less than devoted to my conservative family values?

Years ago I remember my mother worrying incessantly about whether or not her slip was showing. Of course, ladies always worried about those things—at least they did when I was a girl. These days they sometimes dress in fashions that purposely show their slips, but back then we were mortified to have any hint of such things revealed in public. I remember so many times standing in the women's restrooms only to hear a complete stranger ask my mother, "Is my slip showing?"

Well, I'm here today to ask you, "Is your Christianity showing?" Have you let down the undergarment of salvation enough that you reveal to others around you the basis for your foundation? Or have you hidden your faith away, neatly covering it over with a designer fashion.

Sometimes we wear Christian DuJour. You know the fashion. That's the one we put on for the days of the week when we have to go to church or some other Christian function. We look smartly dressed in just the right style. We walk the walk and talk the talk, but when we're out of there and safely hiding back home, we slip back into our regular clothes and save those designer ones for Sunday.

The trouble with Christian DuJour fashions is that nobody outside of those church functions knows we are Christians. We hide our beliefs for fear of retribution from an unimpressed world or simply keep quiet to avoid confrontation. Or worse yet, we don't want to have to explain why we believe what we believe, because we don't know for sure why we believe it.

Often we find ourselves in the position of worrying whether our undergarments of Christ are sticking out offensively to the view of those around us. We've adopted the attitude that the world has thrust upon us: Keep quiet; say nothing; make no one uncomfortable. We worry so much about offending someone with our faith that our faith remains well hidden, buried under layers of worldviews and politically correct behavior.

Is your Christianity showing? If Jesus came back today and had to identify His own people by nothing more than attitude and actions, would He know that you were His? The Bible says the wheat is growing up with the weeds. If we're wheat, we don't want to imitate and clothe ourselves in the fashions of the weeds. We need to be clearly recognized for who we are, and more important, we need to be recognized for *whose* we are. We belong to the King of Kings. The Mighty God. The Everlasting Father.

Instead of hiding our Christianity under the worldly designer rags of complacency, apathy, and self-comfort, let's get a little goofy—a little crazy. Let's hike up that hem on the garment of conservative indifference and let Jesus be revealed. We just might start a new trend in the church—in the body of Christ. We just might start to be recognized as the precious, priceless pieces of work that we are: designer fashions by the Designer of the universe himself.

Isaiah 43:1 says, "Fear not, for I have redeemed you; I have called you by name, you are mine" (RSV).

God's designer label is stamped firmly on your heart. Wear your faith proudly. Let your Christianity show. Let Jesus be the first and last thing people see in you. You just might be surprised at the reactions.

13

Keeping Pace

Have you ever watched children at the mall as they walk with their parents? You see the tiny toddlers who yearn for independence. You can find the older children who run back and forth between store window and parent—constantly wanting, even needing to show Mom and Dad yet another new toy or game. There are even the seemingly disinterested teens who appear to be enduring the trip only for how it will benefit them in the long run.

The other day when I was at the mall, I observed several parents and their children. The first was a frazzled mother who had a child on either side of her. She struggled to hold on to her purse, a store purchase, and the hands of her daughter and son. She was in a hurry, that much was obvious. She wasn't looking to the left or the right. Her vision was fixed straight ahead.

One child was crying and tripping every few steps. She couldn't keep up the pace her mother had set, and so she appeared to be dragged down the mall. The boy, a little bit taller and longer-legged, was running beside his mother to keep up. He was panting for breath and calling out to her to stop. The mother angrily snapped at her son and told him to stop whining, that they were in a hurry.

Been there. Done that.

It was a rather humbling experience as I thought of how many times I've raced my own children from place to place. I watched this woman until she reached the exit and took her children out of the mall. The situation left me saddened and thoughtful. How many times had I been so focused on myself that I'd caused my children to suffer as they struggled to keep up with me? How many times had I been public with my anger and frustration so that others could see how I had treated my little ones?

Next, there was a man with a little girl. She wasn't very old, probably less than two. She held tightly to his hand, and he walked very slowly. Her tiny steps were five or six to his one. But instead of getting after her for her slow pace, he encouraged her.

"Come on, sweetie, you're doing great. Just a few more steps and we'll be there."

The little girl laughed and babbled words I couldn't quite hear. The man smiled and took obvious pleasure in her progress.

"You're doing so good. What a good girl!"

Have you ever wished you could hear God say those words to you? "Come on, just a few more steps. You're doing so well. What a good girl!" The affirmation of this little girl's father was important to her attitude and outlook, just as the negative attitude of the mother with her children had greatly affected their response.

The last child I observed was tired and clearly worn from the day of shopping. He was cranky and miserable, and finally his mother picked him up and soothed him. She carried him from that point on, and he settled down in her arms and immediately came to a place of peace.

The expression of comfort on his face was not one of having been given his way, it was one of sheer rest. He let go of the misery and snuggled into his mother's arms—safe and secure.

It reminded me of that great old hymn "Leaning On the Everlasting Arms." Elisha Hoffman penned the words: "Leaning, leaning, safe and secure from all alarms; Leaning, leaning, leaning on the everlasting arms."

The peace suggested in that hymn is exactly what this child found in his mother's embrace.

Isaiah 46:4 says, "Even to your old age and gray hairs I am he, I am he who will sustain you. I have made you and I will carry you; I will sustain you and I will rescue you."

That verse blesses my heart in ways I can't even begin to put on paper. The very idea that our heavenly Father, our Abba, will carry us, sustain us, rescue us. Like a loving father who offers each of us encouragement along the walk, God is also good to remind us that we need never worry about coming to the place where we collapse on the walk.

I remember a time when I was in Skagway, Alaska. Several people were going to make a long-distance hike to see some of the historical sites. I really wanted to go, but not being a real athletic person, I doubted I could make the eighteen-mile round trip along the rough and rocky course. So I didn't go.

I think a lot of times in life, we find ourselves up against a similar situation. We see a goal, or something comes to us as advantageous to our circumstance, yet we lack the energy or the ability to go forward. We see the distance and the path, and we know that in our own strength, we simply aren't capable of meeting the requirements.

That rocky path might well be a marriage that has many pitfalls and boulders strewn across the way. You might have worked hard to clear the path, only to find a rockslide pouring down around the next bend.

The road might seem easy enough—a straight, flat walk—but the distance is too great, and exhaustion overtakes you. Your generally sweet-natured teen suddenly turns angry and confrontational. You strive to go the distance, to keep up, but you aren't physically capable, and you collapse.

Sometimes the path seems clear of debris and fairly short distance-wise, but the weight of the burden we carry is so great that even a few steps become laborious. Try picking up your refrigerator and walking a few feet! Even if you could lift it, moving it would be an entirely different matter. Burdens are like that. Sometimes we're able to hoist them on our backs, but then we find the weight too great to go any farther.

God tells us in Isaiah that we don't have to worry about the path or the debris or the weight of our burdens. He says that even to our old age He will sustain us. Not only that, but God has promised to carry us. There's no condition on that. It doesn't say, "Now, after you've given it all you've got and have fallen apart without a single ounce of strength left, THEN I'll carry you." God says nothing about your desperation or need; He merely says, "Hey, I made you and I will carry you!"

It doesn't mean that God wants us to be invalids. It doesn't mean we aren't to work for Him—to strive to be living examples of Christ to the world around us. Backing up a few verses in Isaiah 46, God speaks of carrying the entire house of Jacob—all of Israel. It wasn't that God didn't want His people to set out in faith and work for Him, He just offered the reassurance that they would never walk alone.

You won't walk alone either.

Like the father of the toddler in my story, God is right alongside, offering encouragement and pleasure in us as we strive to keep pace with Him. Like the mother with the exhausted boy, God is promising He'll sustain us, carry us, rescue us. We don't have to be afraid that we can't make the journey in our own strength, because God never once asked us to.

We're a proud and stubborn generation. We long for self-accomplishment, and we set lofty goals and aspire to do wonderful things. Sometimes those things are based on good and loving motives. Sometimes they're selfish and self-promoting. The world snaps at us like the mother with her two children. Sometimes the world half drags us along, forcing us to keep a pace we were never intended to walk. Often the world motivates anger and frustration in our hearts, because the demand is too great. We haven't the strength or the ability to do what is required. But the world is in too great a hurry to see our need, much less to care.

But your Father cares. He isn't asking you to run the race alone. He isn't demanding that you keep pace. No, our Abba is standing right before us with open arms. He's smiling in affirmation to let us know that the very best thing we can do is trust Him to sustain and to rescue.

"I have made you, and I will carry you!"

What beautiful words of hope. We aren't in this alone. We don't have to worry about the world's pace. God has a better plan. He has a Father's heart and strong, warm, everlasting arms. We can be "safe and secure from all alarms."

The alternative is obvious. Go it alone in your own strength. Or go in His strength—in His arms. Don't make it harder than it has to be. The best choice is pretty clear.

14

Thank-You Notes

I have a thank-you letter to write, and I don't quite know how to begin it. You see, this letter is going to someone who hasn't always made me very happy. Sometimes we've been at odds; in fact, sometimes we haven't been on good speaking terms. I've been angry and hurt and not always very kind toward the recipient of this note. I've unfairly judged Him, hurt Him, and on more than one occasion questioned His actions as they related to my life.

On the other hand, I owe Him my life.

His name is Jesus Christ.

Sometimes it really amazes me that Jesus would put up with someone like me. I've been stubborn and hardhearted, and there have been times, I'm ashamed to say, that my very actions have denied Him. I owe Him a lot more than a thank-you note, but do you know what? It's a good place to start.

Do you remember in the Bible where Jesus is returning to

Jerusalem in triumph? The account in Luke 19 tells of the people greeting Jesus as He comes down the road. "The whole crowd of disciples began joyfully to praise God in loud voices for all the miracles they had seen: 'Blessed is the king who comes in the name of the Lord! Peace in heaven and glory in the highest!' "

The people were overwhelmed with the happiness and excitement of seeing Jesus. They had witnessed the things He had done. They had seen Him raise the dead to life. They had seen Him feed huge crowds with a few fish and a few loaves of bread. The blind had been given sight, the deaf could hear, and the lame could walk. The crowd couldn't keep quiet. They had to praise Him. They had to shout to the Lord in gratitude.

The Pharisees weren't thrilled about this. Pharisees seldom are. They didn't appreciate Jesus' way of doing things. They didn't like His "love revolution." They were so put out by this, in fact, that they turned to Jesus and demanded, "Teacher, rebuke your disciples."

Can't you just see it? The people are delirious. They are singing and shouting praises to their Lord. They recognize the power and the hope in Jesus, even if they don't fully understand that He's the Messiah they've been waiting for. They want to tap into that power—if only for the moment.

The other night on television, I saw a young woman who has become a pop star. She gave a homecoming concert, complete with the whole town turning out to throw her a parade. People of all ages gathered. Children screamed and waved banners. Teenagers shouted her name and danced to her music. Even the hometown adults cheered to see one of their own having done so well.

It was quite a phenomenon for this little town. It would have been quite an ordeal for a big town. Now try to imagine quelling this group. Try to imagine making them be quiet. Even if this girl had raised her hands and pleaded with them for silence, they wouldn't have accommodated her. They were caught up in a spirit of praise.

Sadly enough, I think we often reserve this kind of joy for pop stars and political figures. We see what the world honors and respects, and we just get caught up in the spirit of it. We lose ourselves, and we lose touch with the one we really ought to be praising.

Go back to Luke and the Pharisees commanding Jesus to quiet His followers. I imagine Jesus looking at these men with just a hint of a grin. The kind of look a person has when he knows a secret that no one else knows.

Jesus says, "I tell you . . . if they keep quiet, the stones will cry out."

Now, that's a praise party that would knock your socks off. Imagine all of creation joining in with the rocks to offer Jesus praise.

"If they keep quiet, the stones will cry out."

What about us? We've seen Jesus at work. Maybe we haven't seen the dead raised, although there was a woman in my church for whom the doctors gave no hope. You probably know someone like her, someone who beat the odds of cancer or some other life-threatening situation. Then again, maybe you saw the dead raised to life in the form of a drug addict who came clean or a prodigal returned home.

Maybe we haven't seen the lame walk, although I saw a medical documentary on prosthetic appliances and watched as a young woman ran marathons on a man-made foot. Does it count as a miracle when it's a matter of God giving wisdom and knowledge, insight and imagination to mere mortals?

I've seen God provide food when there was nothing left in the cupboard. I've seen money come in an unmarked envelope when my children needed medicine. I've seen storms dissipate, wayward children come home, and hope in the midst of hopelessness. I think I qualify as one of those people who has seen the miracles of God, and if you're honest about it, you probably qualify too. It really doesn't matter what we label it—it's God at work.

So what about it?

Why do I bring it up? Why do I bother to write it out on the pages of this book? Because I think we've become indifferent in offering our praise. I think we're relying on the rocks to cry out. God has provided and performed as He always has in His unchanging state, and yet we have fallen short of recognizing His wonders and blessings. Some of us owe God a thank-you note. I know I do.

I'm ashamed when I think of the praise party thrown for a young pop star, yet know that few people would turn out if I threw a parade for Jesus. I'm saddened when praise and prayer services are offered and only a handful of the congregation bothers to show up. I'm grieved deep down in my heart when people say there is no evidence of God or that there is no God.

A pastor once said that one of the first requirements of a heart of praise is to recognize the gifts you've been given. Makes sense to me. Imagine trying to thank someone for a birthday present when you don't even know what they've given you, or *if* they've given you something. We have only to open our eyes and look around us to see what God has done—what He is offering us. If we can't see anything else, then we must see Jesus. Jesus was and is God's best and finest gift.

Have you thanked God lately for His Son?

What about God's creation? The beauty of the mountains and oceans, the prairies and forests. What about the awesome wonders of reproduction? Of animals that give birth without anyone to aid them, of plants and cross-pollination? What about our own intricate human bodies—bodies so complicated and detailed that doctors and scientists are still trying to figure out what makes us tick? What about our possessions, our jobs, our education, and even the ability to read and write?

I challenge you today to write a thank-you note to Jesus. Pick up that pen and get to work. Make a list and watch it grow as you open the eyes of your heart. Because as much as I think it would be really radical to hear the rocks praising God, I'd much rather we human beings share in the joy and praise Him ourselves.

But just in case I forget, I'm going to keep a rock close by. You just never know.

15

Not Responsible for Damage

R ecently I've been assaulted by a number of "not responsible for damage" signs. They're posted at my grocery store: "Not responsible for damage done by grocery carts." They're hanging at the playground: "Not responsible for injuries caused while playing on equipment." I've even found them at the car wash, where the management proclaims: "Not liable for damage done to vehicle."

We are a people who shirk from the responsibility of accepting blame. We learn it early on. For instance, one time my daughters decided we needed a fire in the fireplace. The only problem was, we didn't have a fireplace. The solution? Stuff paper in the furnace and see if the pilot light could create a blaze.

"Who's responsible for this?" we asked.

"Not me," they cried in unison.

Even the early stories in the Bible deal with shirking responsibility. Eve blames the serpent, Adam blames Eve, and then he indirectly blames God: "The woman you gave me . . ." You can just hear the implication of his heart: "If you hadn't saddled me with this woman, I wouldn't be in this fix right now."

Every day we hear people denying responsibility. We hear it come out of the mouths of murderers: "I didn't know what I was doing. . . . I wasn't thinking right." We hear it from our politicians when things go amiss in the government: "This is the fault of [the other political party]." We see it when children run amuck and damage property and each other. The schools blame the parents; the parents blame society; and society turns its back and blames the government for tying its hands or for being too liberal with the interpretation of the Constitution.

We have a responsibility phobia.

And why not? Accepting responsibility means someone might hold us accountable, and if we can escape that, we are a much happier people. At least we think we are.

My mother taught me something when I was very young—a philosophy of life, if you will. I've passed this philosophy down to my children, although I'm not sure they've entirely bought into it. My mother said, "Always accept responsibility for the things you do, bad or good. When you make a mistake or create a problem, be the first one to acknowledge it. That way when something goes wrong and they come to you and it isn't your fault, they'll be more inclined to believe you. After all, they'll remember you always admitted to your mistakes in the past."

And it generally works. It saved me in sticky situations more than once. Holding myself accountable to those around me gave me liberty. Accepting responsibility for the things that were truly my responsibility set me free.

Most people don't believe that. They look at responsibility as shackles binding their feet and hands. The man who fathers a child out of wedlock sees accepting responsibility as taking on more than he bargained for. He might end up with a wife and a baby to take care of. The woman who finds herself pregnant might have to face public humiliation and ultimate responsibility for a baby she hadn't planned on. Both are weighed down by accepting responsibility for their actions and choices, when, in fact, they could have enjoyed liberty had they accepted responsibility several paces back and held each other accountable to remain pure. And even facing up to the event of an unplanned, out-of-wedlock pregnancy can eventually merit liberty as well. We do a lot of growing up and gaining of wisdom in accepting responsibility. And with wisdom comes liberty.

How about it? Do you know someone who might as well be wearing one of those signs? NOT RESPONSIBLE FOR DAMAGE . . . You can smile here. I know you understand. I have several faces that come to mind. Sadly enough, I have to include my own. There have been times when I've not wanted to be accountable, and I might as well have declared to the world that I was not responsible for the damage I caused.

The blame game is so very convenient. As I mentioned, we're taught it from a very early age. It's second nature, or better yet, first nature. Pass the buck, let somebody else take the fall, let someone else pay the price.

Guess what? Someone else did.

I imagine Jesus standing before the Father in love and compassion. "They're weak," He might say of us on earth. "Sin has weighed them down. Why not let me take that weight? I'll be responsible for their damage."

On the cross, Jesus might as well have worn a sign that read, RESPONSIBLE FOR IT ALL.

"That's right. I did it. Right here—me. If you must blame someone, pin it here to this cross." I can see His loving eyes so full of pain, His heart so full of love. He didn't deserve to be held accountable or responsible for our sins, but He knew we could never bear it alone. He knew if left to our own devices, we would be hopelessly awash in the blame game and the guilt and the bondage of our frail humanity.

Even today Jesus reaches out His arms in an offering of love. "Accept me as Savior," He pleads, "and I will make you right before God the Father. I'll take the responsibility; I'll bear the sins of the world."

It doesn't mean we're off the hook, that we don't have any responsibility in this situation. Because we do. We have to yield to Him. To accept His way of doing things. To accept Him.

What are you shirking today? What damage are you refusing responsibility for? Maybe you spoke harsh words in anger, injuring and inflicting pain in verbal firefights, leaving a battlefield of wounded in your wake. It could be you caused division among friends or family. Perhaps you even lied to make yourself look better, all the while damaging the reputation of someone else.

NOT RESPONSIBLE FOR DAMAGE? That's a lie. We *are* responsible. We will all give an account to our Father in heaven, just as the Bible says. Frankly, I know my own weaknesses, and I'd rather stand with Jesus as my advocate than without Him. How about you? We aren't without responsibility, but we have one who will go before us. We have a Savior and counselor and intercessor in Jesus Christ. Don't let His love slip by you. Accept responsibility. Accept Him.

16

Be Prepared

T he old adage from my scouting days was *Be prepared*. This motto has followed me from grade school into adulthood, from dating to marriage, from childbirth to the death of loved ones. Had I been in charge of Patton's push across France, he would never have run out of gasoline. If I had been in charge of the *Titanic*, there would have been plenty of lifeboats for everyone and then some. When I plan family get-togethers, there is always enough food to feed a small army, and when I travel, the kitchen sink goes in before anything else. Being prepared has at times become a bit obsessive with me, but then again, it's a biblical principle. So why not obsess on something that comes right out of the Word?

Jesus tells his disciples in Matthew 24:42–44, "Therefore keep watch, because you do not know on what day your Lord will come. But understand this: If the owner of the house had known at what time of night the thief was coming, he would have kept watch and would not have let his house be broken into. So you also must be ready, because the Son of Man will come at an hour when you do not expect him."

Jesus was saying, "Be prepared." It's a pretty important statement. Have you given it any thought?

Having lived in Kansas most of my life, we had a springtime routine that involved checking batteries in flashlights and the weather radio, all while keeping an eye to the sky. Springtime in Kansas is tornado season, and we take our tornadoes very seriously.

From my first memory of this springtime ritual, I knew that the occasion merited much attention and concentration. My mother gave us all a job to do in order to prepare for the season. I usually had the job of sweeping out the basement. Often this floor was nothing more than packed dirt—but let me tell you, it was the best-swept dirt floor in Kansas. Sometimes I had the job of making sure there were pillows or blankets available for those late night storms that might see us spending the evening in the basement.

I remember my mother having my sister and me prepare our "important" things. This was to be a little bag of mementos, do-dads that meant more to us than the run-of-the-mill possession. She didn't do this to teach us to care overly about our things, but rather to get our minds focused on something other than the weather. It was a form of preparation that gave us freedom when the storm actually descended upon us. It allowed us to simply make a run for the basement with our little bag in hand. It gave us a tiny bit of control over the impending doom. Preparation invested us in the outcome.

Kansas tornadoes, for those of you who are unfamiliar, range all up and down the Fujita Scale. The Fujita Scale is used to rate the intensity of a tornado by examining the damage caused after the tornado has passed over a man-made structure.

F1 is a small tornado, while F5s are those devastating fist-of-God kind of storms that usually leave entire cities devastated in their wake. F5s scourge pavement off highways and rip houses off foundations and leave kindling in their place. You don't want to scoff at any tornado, but you especially don't want to take an F5 for granted.

The weather bureau is pretty good at giving us a little warning. In Kansas, our worst storms generally came in the late afternoon or early evening. So when the elements were right, the weather bureau might put us in a tornado watch in the early afternoon. It's a declaration of preparation. It's a call to go on alert—to be watchful. To stand ready.

Now, some folks never concern themselves with these watches. They simply go about their business as usual. You've probably seen them. They're usually the ones on the television news telling their story of being lifted up into the tornado while driving down the interstate. They almost always end their testimony with the words "I had no idea it was even coming."

They weren't prepared. But they could have been. The alert had been given, and while there was no way to know whether the storm would form and come on that day or that particular hour, they were warned to be ready.

Jesus tells us to be ready—to keep watch for His return. We don't know when He will come; we have no specific date to put on our calendar. In fact, Jesus tells us He'll come at an hour we don't expect Him.

But what's important to know and remember is that He is coming. We've been warned. The alert has gone out. Jesus is coming back. Will you be ready?

In Matthew 25, Jesus tells the parable of the wise and the foolish virgins. These women are waiting for their bridegroom to show up. They all have their lamps, but only the wise ones thought to prepare just in case the night got long. When the cry is given that the bridegroom is on his way, the foolish virgins realize they have very little oil left. They aren't prepared. And because they aren't prepared, they miss out.

While the foolish virgins go off to buy oil for their lamps, the bridegroom comes and takes the wise virgins in to the wedding banquet. By the time the foolish virgins get back with their oil, the door has been shut to them. The bridegroom rejects them.

Jesus is the bridegroom, and we, like it or not, are the foolish and the wise brides-to-be. Some of us are ready for our groom to come and take us to the wedding banquet. But others aren't. Some of you out there fear the upcoming feast. You know you aren't ready. You know your lamp is running low on oil. You didn't plan to be remiss. You didn't plan to ignore the Holy Spirit's prompting. But . . .

Maybe you stand ready with a full lamp and an industrial-size barrel of oil alongside you, but you've never bothered to tell your sister or your friends that they need oil too. Maybe they don't know the bridegroom is coming back for them. They can't be prepared if they don't know what's required.

At the end of the parable of the virgins, Jesus again says, "Therefore keep watch, because you do not know the day or the hour." He's talking about His return. He's talking about coming back for His bride—the church. We don't know when that will be, but we can rest assured that the day *is* coming.

Be prepared!

How? First, see to your own lamp. Set your heart on God and seek Him for the oil of life. Search the Scriptures for a refilling of your lamp's reservoir. Seek the Holy Spirit to kindle the flame that will light your way. If your own lamp isn't in order, you can't help anyone else with their lamp.

When your heart is right before God, and your life is fixed on seeking His will, then help your sister with her lamp. Get together to pray and encourage one another. Have lunch with an unsaved friend and let the Holy Spirit illuminate the setting. Pray fervently for those who choose darkness, and remember God is in the business of lighting dark paths. Start a Bible study. Start a neighborhood teatime and invite your neighbors to hear the Good News. And if the adults aren't interested, shine the light of Jesus to their children when they come over to play with your kids.

Preparation makes the road much easier to travel. Be prepared! Jesus is coming back. There's no question about that. It's just a matter of time. Will you be ready?

17

See What I'm Saying

When our daughter Julie was just five or six, she came home from school babbling in her excited way about her day. My husband, already busy at the table with one of his projects, listened to her talk while he worked. He asked the right questions and listened as best he could while continuing with the tasks he had in hand. He thought he was doing a really good job, until our daughter took his face in her hands and turned him toward herself.

"Daddy, you can't see what I'm saying."

My husband had to smile at her words and put down what he was doing. Sometimes we need to see what someone is saying.

Jesus knew this. I believe that's why He told parables. The people needed the picture in order to "see what He was saying." People today are no different. Oftentimes the world is full of words and noises, and no one ever really understands or hears the meaning of those sounds.

I don't think it's just a matter of people not listening. I think it has more to do with the sound of their own pain and worry being louder than the decibels of the information coming to them. The roaring of their own hurt blocks out the words of comfort and truth—words they most definitely need to hear.

Take, for instance, a woman I know. She labored long and hard to be a good wife and mother. She gave of herself in such an unselfish way that people actually stood by in amazement. People other than the members of her own family, that is. As she began to break down and wear out, as her own needs could no longer be put off, she asked her loved ones for help. But no one heard.

My friend tried to keep things moving forward. She tried to continue being a good wife and mother. She tried to see to it that the laundry was done and the house picked up. She worked her hardest to see that the kids had all they needed and most of what they wanted, and still no one heard her cries for help. No one heard her pleading for some affection, some warmth, some acceptance of who she was rather than what she did. Not one member of her family attempted to meet her needs. Her kids were too busy, and her husband, well, he simply didn't have a clue.

No one could see what she was saying. No one, that is, until a stranger came into the picture. He listened. He cared. He made my friend feel special.

Sadly, the worst happened. My friend clung to this new hope and found herself in the middle of an affair. Not long after that her marriage fell apart; her kids rejected her, and most of her friends and family turned away from her in disgust and anger. She had cried out for help, for love and understanding, and no one could see what she was saying. The words were obscured because the focus was on their own needs rather than on hers.

All she needed was for someone to see what she was saying. She needed to have a reason to hope—to believe that someone loved her as much as she loved them. Have you ever felt that way? Have you ever stood in the middle of an auditorium full of people and just wished, prayed, that someone would understand? Was there ever a moment in time when you reached out, threw a party in your own honor, so to speak—and nobody came?

The loneliest feeling in the world is to be desperately vulnerable, open and honest about your need, and still no one extends a comforting hand. No one will go the distance with you.

Jesus knew that feeling. He went to the Garden to pray before his crucifixion. He took some good friends with Him. Peter and James and John. He said to them, "My soul is overwhelmed with sorrow to the point of death. Stay here and keep watch with me" (Matthew 26:38).

Has your soul been overwhelmed with sorrow to the point of death? Mine has. I find this verse so very precious. Our Savior knows what it is to be overwhelmed with grief. He knows just how bad *bad* can be. And, because Jesus experienced this deep abiding pain, He can see what we're saying when we pray in our pain.

I tried my best to help my friend when her sorrow overwhelmed her. I tried to pray with her—to listen to her—to love her. It was something given from the heart, but it wasn't enough. The people she really needed got up and walked away.

But the Savior she needed, didn't.

In her desperation, my friend reached out to Jesus, and He came to keep watch with her. He didn't demand she perform for Him. He didn't require she first prove her worth. He came when she had nothing left to offer. He came when she was sorrowed to the point of death—lost in her sin and misery.

And Jesus will come to you as well. He will walk the path with you. He will bear your sorrows and nurse your wounds. Jesus will see what you are saying, and better yet, He will see it with the eyes of the heart. The eyes of Jesus' heart are fixed on the needs of His loved ones. He longs to be there for you—He longs for you to come to Him.

Jesus loves you.

Jesus honestly and truly loves you. And His love can see the details the world fails to see. His love will heal the pain that no one else knows or understands. He doesn't care where you've been or what you've done—He only asks that you come home. Like the father of the prodigal, it only matters that you come.

What are you waiting for?

18

The Fleshly Wrestling Association

Picture, if you will, grown men cavorting in leotards and capes. Masks or elaborate makeup shield their identity. No, it's not the ballet, it's a televised wrestling match. These men stand toe-to-toe, matching brawn for brawn, blow for blow. The crowds pay outrageous money to see these spectacles, and the television announcers make more noise and fuss than women in labor.

Watching wrestlers throw each other into the ropes or do the death slam or whatever they call it is not exactly my cup of tea, but I found the example useful.

So often I've tried to wrestle in the flesh to solve my problems. My opponents are often unknown to me until I've gone several rounds, but usually they have specific names and elaborate trappings. They come in the guise of friends or minor conflicts. They come flying at me from every direction, refusing to yield the floor, threatening my welfare and security, slamming me up against the ropes.

Sometimes the matches are short and simple, and I easily come out the victor. Other times the fights are long and arduous, lasting well into the night. I've lain awake entire nights battling problems that seemed so overwhelming that they were wrestling the life right out of me. I've come face-to-face with situations where my flesh demanded retribution, reward, revenge. While at the same time, my spirit pleaded with me to turn to my Father's interests rather than self-interests. Some battles were won, and some were lost, and just like flesh and blood battles, these spiritual battles left their wounds and injuries.

Sound familiar? Have you ever labored in your own strength to fight a spiritual conflict? Ephesians 6:12 states, "For our struggle is not against flesh and blood, but against the rulers, against the authorities, against the powers of this dark world and against the spiritual forces of evil in the heavenly realms."

Our struggle isn't against flesh and blood, but we certainly fight our battles as though they were. We fight selfish fights, noble fights, even righteous fights. We battle for our own cause and for the cause of our loved ones. I can't begin to tell you the number of times I've taken up offenses for my friends and family. Wound someone I love, and you wound me. It's a part of the fierce loyalty I feel for those whom I care about. It can also turn to sin rather quickly.

We wrestle against all kinds of problems—spiritual battles of will that seem to grow darker and more demanding by the minute. We fight and fuss and push and strain against the Enemy and still we find ourselves bloodied and worn.

We battle financial worries, we fight against lies told about us, and we wage war against the pain of rejection. Spiritually, we battle against having our own way, against changing lifelong habits of destruction, against giving ourselves over to sin because it seems more self-gratifying than purity. We struggle to the point of losing sleep, losing weight, and losing our minds. We fight a battle in the flesh that has no basis in flesh.

Spiritual battles are nothing new. Eve faced one at the hand of the serpent. Saul was convinced putting an end to David would solve his own spiritual problems. The Pharisees and Sadducees were certain the spiritual well-being and the healing of the Jewish people could be resolved by killing Jesus.

Spiritual battles come in every shape and form. They come in misunderstanding. Satan loves to work in this form. He uses misunderstanding as an oil painter uses canvas and brushes. It's one of his finest mediums. Misunderstanding can start in the most innocent way and then snowball into tragedy.

Another of Satan's favorite tactics is the craft of assigning motive, or judging. Christians are some of the harshest judges of people and their sins. Satan loves this. He uses it to divide us and to destroy the foundation of love and hope that Jesus has given us.

Picture a woman fretting and worrying about why her husband hasn't come home from work. It's late, and he's well overdue. Add to this a rocky background for their marriage. The husband had once been a drinker and a womanizer. No matter that he's turned his life over to God and hasn't carried on in this way for more than a year. The wife begins to judge her husband for his tardiness.

"I'll bet he's slipped into his old ways," she says. "He's probably at a bar right now." Her anger grows as she looks at the clock. He's more than two hours late, and memories of his past mistakes are hurtling fiery darts her way. She plays judge and jury, condemning her mate for actions that may or may not be true. Another half hour passes before her weary husband drags in through the door. "There was an accident—a tire blew—the car went off the road," he explains, but instead of worrying about her husband's condition or whether he was even involved, the wife is angry and filled with doubts.

The battle is on.

The spiritual damage is done.

Another wrestling match begins because of worry. Worry is a spiritual battle I know well. I have often battled in the flesh to try to defeat worry. I've rushed around to complete a task, worked an extra job to make ends meet, juggled important priorities to the back burner in order to take care of ones that seemed more important.

At the end of the day I drag around in a weariness suggestive of having engaged in intense physical labor. When, in fact, it's my spirit that has been defeated and worn. I've chosen to wrestle in the flesh, and now I'm paying the price. My battle was never against fleshly opponents, but it's taken its toll on my flesh, nevertheless.

In this damaged and wounded state, I finally turn to my real source of strength. The source I should have gone to in the first place. But I often ignore Him until I've exhausted my own possibilities. Jesus is the source.

Sometimes we forget that He's already fought the battle for us. He took the misunderstandings, concerns, worries, and fears, along with every insult, false judgment, and undeserved condemnation, and allowed them to be nailed with Him to the cross. We needn't take them back, but so often we do. We struggle and strain and fight and wrestle, and all the time we suffer. But we don't have to.

Jesus is in the business of spiritual wrestling matches. He knows the opponent better than we can hope to. He knows the Enemy and his moves—his tricks and his conflicts. Jesus won't ask you to fight in the flesh what so clearly can only be battled in the spirit. What Jesus will do, however, is require you to get out of the wrestling ring and leave the match to Him. He's your champion—your defender—your hope. So instead of wearing ourselves out wrestling with an adversary who is after our lifeblood, why not send Jesus in to do battle instead?

How is this accomplished? First, you must believe that Jesus will go to bat for you, believe that He wants to stand as your champion and protector. Jesus has already won the victory, and Satan has no power over you. Do you believe this?

Second, stop jumping to conclusions when misunderstandings and questionable motives come into play. When someone says something that grates, when someone's tone sounds accusing or harsh, rather than respond or assign motives, pray through the matter. Ask God to give you a right heart. Ask God to give you grace to endure touchy situations without speaking out and causing more trouble. Whatever you do, don't go back into the ring.

And last of all, stop thinking you have to do everything—face every battle—on your own. You have a champion who will go forward, a loving Savior who has already taken your place on the cross, where it really mattered. Do you doubt that He will intercede for you in the minor conflicts of daily life when He so willingly gave His life for you?

Take off those wrestling boots and that mask. Take off the super-avenger cape. Reach out your hand and take hold of the King of Kings. Then sit back and rest in the divine nature of God's protection, while Jesus takes Satan to the mat. The bell has sounded. A new round is about to begin. What's it going to be? You, wrestling in the flesh? Or Jesus, stepping in on your behalf?

19

Does God Reach Back?

With the exception of two years when we lived in Dallas, Texas, I spent the first fourteen years of my life in a church that was pretty low-tech and even-keeled. We didn't clap or sing any song that hadn't been approved for the hymnal, and we certainly didn't have guitars or drums in the worship service. In fact, I'm almost certain someone told me that drums were the devil's playthings, and it was probably for this reason I was never given one as a toy. Then again, it could be I made enough noise on my own, making a drum unnecessary.

We were so calm in our worship that you rarely saw anyone raise a hand during the singing. Oh, once in a while, one of the little old ladies who didn't have to worry about what people thought would raise one arm toward the ceiling during a particularly moving chorus of "I Surrender All." But otherwise there wasn't a whole lot of visible worship going on.

When I was five years old, I remember standing in church singing "Amazing Grace," when one of the older women raised her shaky right hand. Now, on this particular occasion, a little girl in front of me just happened to pose a question. I can still hear her.

"Momma, is that lady reaching up to touch God's hand?"

Her mother, ever patient, leaned down and whispered, "Yes. That's exactly what she's doing."

"Does God reach back?" the child asked.

Good question, I thought. Does He? If so, why aren't we all raising our hands? And if not, why not? Doesn't God want to touch us? My five-year-old mind ran rampant. I waited eagerly for her mother's answer and leaned forward ever so slightly to get the scoop.

"Of course He does," the mother replied.

I breathed a sigh of relief. But then I got to thinking about it. I mean, I'd never seen my mother or father or grandmother raise their hands to touch God. Was there something wrong with them? Didn't they want to touch Him?

The next week at church, I learned that the same old lady had died. Again my mind sorted through the details, and I decided that raising your hand was kind of like a signal to God. It suggested you were ready to go—sort of an intergalactic, divine thumb out to hitch a ride to heaven. No wonder people didn't raise their hands to God. If you did, you got snatched up and taken away.

After that I started watching folks carefully. If anyone I cared about raised their hand, I wanted to be sure to give them a hug good-bye. I didn't know exactly how quick God would reach back and grab them, but I wanted to be on the safe side. I didn't have a whole lot of trouble with the situation. Like I said, we were a pretty easygoing, but stuffy-formal church.

As I grew older, I came to reconsider the idea and realized, mainly because people weren't disappearing as much as hands were going up, it was a bit off base. I figured what I'd heard that mother tell her child was true. Folks were reaching up to God, and God most likely reached back. But I wasn't sure why they were doing it.

Now, I had given my heart to Jesus at the age of six, but I have to be honest. I did it mostly out of fear of hell and the awful judgment of a long-bearded God. Beards scared me anyway at that age, and when my Sunday school teacher suggested that the way to get on God's good side was to accept His Son as Savior, well, I was all for it.

And, of course, I loved God. You had to. Otherwise He might come down and take issue with you. But I wanted to love God too, because my folks had instilled in me a love of His creation and a belief in His mercy and love for us. But even with this, I still wasn't sure why I would want to reach out and touch God.

I pondered the situation long and hard. Believe me, when I get to pondering, the wheels keep spinning until I'm satisfied with the conclusion. I figured there was something to this that I just wasn't getting. Maybe the mother had been wrong. Maybe people weren't reaching up to touch God, but rather putting out a hand to ward Him off. A kind of ducking system that suggested acceptance of fault on the part of the sinner, but the desire to deflect the blows of correction. It seemed possible, at least in theory.

During my teens we changed churches, and the people were a bit more open with their hand-raising. Some waved them in the air as if they were trying to get God's attention, while others barely bent their elbows and held their hands up. It looked like they'd lost the tray they'd been carrying. Some even raised both hands, and let me tell you, that was a bit startling. It added a whole new aspect to my reasoning. Because now the people looked more like large children, raising their arms to be picked up. Not only this, but they did it when we were singing praise songs and choruses of love. I kind of liked the idea of reaching up to my Abba Father, who by this time was no longer an imposing God on a throne who was waiting to smack me upside the head when I strayed, but rather the one who wanted to love me into repentance.

I no longer worried about whether reaching upward was a signal to beam me up. And I no longer figured it to be a way to keep God from using His mighty right hand to put me in my place. Reaching up seemed a reasonable, tangible act of a child who wanted to be held by her Father. I gave it a try.

I slipped up my right hand as we sang "Blessed Assurance." It felt wonderful. I looked around me and saw a few other hands uplifted, but it wouldn't have mattered if I'd been the only one. I was reaching up to touch my Father's hand. And do you know what?

He does reach back.

20

The Faith of a Mother's Prayer

When I was about eight years old, we moved to Dallas, Texas, so that my father could attend computer school for two years. We had never had a lot of money, but moving robbed my folks of what little comfort they'd had. My father's paycheck was much less than it had been, while the bills were every bit as high. On top of this, my folks had acquired new expenses with the move. The budget was tight. The margin for error was zero.

I remember my folks trying to figure out how to make it all come together. We rented a run-down house in a poorer section of town. My mother often joked that the cockroaches helped us move in. My dad said the bugs were big enough to saddle and ride. My sister and I were fairly oblivious to the worries they suffered, because our folks did a good job of hiding their worry from us.

We made soup out of ketchup and called it fun. We bought five-cent bags of week-old bread and considered it a prized find. We filled the deep-fat fryer with water in order to heat a can of black-eyed peas, because my folks couldn't afford both electricity and gas, and the stove was gas operated. I didn't know we had it all that bad, until we went to bed one Saturday evening, and I heard my mother crying from the other room.

Nothing strikes fear in the heart of a child so easily as hearing a parent cry. When parents cry, you know that something really bad has happened. When parents cry, children cry too. And I did.

The next day we ate what was left of the old, dry bread, feeling blessed by the fact that we could toast it. Feeling like kings, because my dad had brought home packets of jelly from work. We went to church not with full bellies, but not empty ones either. Coming home, however, we knew the truth. There was nothing left. There was no food in the house, and payday was five days away.

Eating and playing were my only real concerns at that age. Now one of the major components of my security was missing. The cupboards were bare.

I don't know if this has ever happened to you, but let me tell you, it's a fearful thing. I remember wondering why we couldn't just go to the store and get some food. It seemed very logical to my eight-year-old mind. Never mind the money part.

I was a fairly astute child and saw the worry in my parents' expressions. I'd heard my mother cry the night before. I knew things weren't good, but I didn't know how to help. I asked my mother what we were going to do, and she said, "Pray."

I had known my mother to be a woman of prayer since my first memories of her. She believed in the power of prayer and had great faith that God would see us through. Her faith became food to my soul.

As she began to pray, I felt my spirit calm. I heard her pray for our meal—the meal that wasn't even there. I heard her thank God for the food He would provide. Then she closed the prayer and looked to each of us. "What do we do now?" I asked.

"We wait for God," she told me.

It was only a few minutes later that someone knocked on our front door. In anticipation of answered prayer, I followed my mother and father to the door. Outside, on the front porch, were several of the new friends we'd made at church. Their arms were full with sacks and bundles of food. Not just cans and packages of unprepared food, but also a hot meal, ready for our consumption.

Loaves and fishes. Ravens bringing bread and meat.

My mother cried, which made me a bit weepy as well. I wasn't sure why she was crying, and it caused me to fear. Seeing me in such a state, she turned and smiled, saying, "Look what God has provided." The words gave me an overwhelming feeling of confidence in the power of prayer. After our friends left the food and had gone, we sat down to a wonderful lunch, and again my mother praised God for His bounty.

"We are sharing a meal of answered prayer," my mother told us.

The thought intrigued me and forever changed my life. Suddenly every Bible story miracle was visible on my table. God sending manna to the Israelites. The boy with his fish and bread lunch being multiplied to thousands. Elijah being fed by the ravens. Every single time God had heard the prayers of the destitute was evidenced in that meal. And even at eight years old, I knew the truth of the power of prayer.

Faith in God, born through answered prayer, is a matter of the heart. It's the quiet prayer whispered at the incubator of a premature infant. It's the elderly woman who puts in her tithe, knowing full well she doesn't have enough to live on. Faith is knowing that God is who He says He is, even when it seems impossible for it to be true. It's the impossible that makes faith so very possible. Because God is a God of impossibilities.

The faith prayers of a godly mother are a thing of wonder. My mother shared her faith with me, and God opened my heart to see the marvel of it all. Food came not by ravens but by loving people who knew what it was to be hungry. Friendship was offered not because of what we could give in return but because they were living out the very essence of Christ through their kindness.

Faith grows when it is fed. It gets fat and sassy when it is shared. Faith and prayer walk hand in hand, believing, when the darkest hour is upon us. Prayer delivers us to the throne room of God. Faith tells us our Father is there—ready and willing to listen. Ready and willing to act.

Maybe faith comes hard to you. A hope in God's promises is far from your ability to reach. Do you long for faith? Do you look at others around you and feel that somehow you're missing the key ingredient? Does prayer seem to be a waste of time? Are you afraid God won't answer—or worse yet, He isn't listening?

Oswald Chambers states in his book *If Ye Shall Ask*, "Our Lord in His teaching regarding prayer never once referred to unanswered prayer; He said God always answers prayer. If our prayers are in the name of Jesus, i.e., in accordance with His nature, the answer will not be in accordance with our nature, but with His. We are apt to forget this, and to say without thinking that God does not always answer prayer."[1]

God always answers our prayers. We must have faith to believe that. Faith is knowing that God can see—that He already has seen—our need and provided for it.

James 2:14–17 says, "What good is it, my brothers, if a man claims to have faith but has no deeds? Can such faith save him? Suppose a brother or sister is without clothes and daily food. If one of you says to him, 'Go, I wish you well; keep warm and well fed,' but does nothing about his physical needs, what good is it? In the same way, faith by itself, if it is not accompanied by action, is dead."

Maybe your faith just needs a little CPR. Maybe the first action that's missing is turning your eyes to heaven and opening your mouth in prayer. Maybe the second action is opening your eyes to the needs around you rather than focusing on your own. A church in Dallas, Texas, rallied to answer the prayers of a godly mother. They didn't know her need, but God did. And because of their action and my mother's prayers, the spiritual life of an eight-year-old girl was forever, profoundly changed.

Loaves and fishes are often the only faith we need to start us on our feast. Loaves of prayer and fishes of hope. They're the only ingredients needed to produce a God-sized feast that's guaranteed to fatten your faith and change your life.

---

[1] Oswald Chambers, *If You Will Ask*, 1989. Used by permission of Discovery House Publishers, Box 3566, Grand Rapids, MI 49501. All rights reserved.

21

Falling Through the Cracks

Once we were staying at a rustic cabin in the mountains of Colorado. The cabin left a little bit to be desired, especially for my thoroughly modern children. My son, however, having the foresight to pack his trusty Legos, made the best of a bad situation. Without television, he was forced to focus on using his imagination—which, if not one of the established spiritual gifts, is surely a gift of the Lord, nevertheless.

Playing with his toys, he suddenly grew agitated, then frantic. "What's wrong?" I questioned, completely in the dark as to why he should be so out of sorts.

"My Lego man fell through the crack in the floor." He struggled and worked to get that little man back, but it was a seemingly impossible task. The crack was just big enough to lose a toy, but not big enough for a boy's hand to reach through. There were very few choices. We could forget the little man, tear up the floor, or utilize some sort of tool for retrieval.

Life in the church body can sometimes be the same way. People fall through the cracks all the time. Good people. Honest people. Tired people. Poor people. They come from all walks of life and have all kinds of stories to tell. They are of every race, culture, color, and gender. They are God's children, and yet they are often forgotten and overlooked by the body of Christ.

Let me give you an example or two. There was a woman I'll call Anna. She was married and had two beautiful children. She was very poor—poverty-stricken—but Anna loved God. Every Sunday she faithfully came to church and brought her two children. Anna's husband wasn't interested in spiritual matters or issues of faith. He chose Sunday for sleeping in and watching football. Anna tried to convince him to join her, but it only turned ugly when she stressed his need for God. Sunday mornings at home soon became a battleground for Anna and her children.

Sunday at church wasn't much better. Anna showed up in clothes that suggested a tour of the secondhand store. Anna couldn't afford to tithe big bucks, but she gave what she could—what she was allowed to give by her husband. Spiritually starving, emotionally spent, and in desperate need of love and friendship, Anna had very little to offer anyone in the church. She was needy, and it was very evident.

Needy people have a way of frightening others. Anna's needs were so great that it probably seemed overwhelming to most people. Week after week she came to church, sat in her Sunday school class, and later in the sanctuary, listening to the sermon, and week after week she went home with scarcely a word spoken to her. She didn't fit in with the married women, and she didn't fit in with the singles. She didn't feel she could attend the couples' Sunday school class, but the only other classes offered for adults were for college age or seniors—neither of which she fit.

Slowly but surely Anna realized she felt worse at church fellow-shipping, or more accurately, watching others fellowship, than she felt by staying home. Little by little, Anna fell through the cracks, and no one even noticed.

Then there was a lovely teenage girl. I'll call her Sarah. Sarah was extremely bright. She was a straight-A student and very mature for her age. When her friends were reading youth books, Sarah was already reading classics, and by the time she was old enough to attend the youth group in her church, Sarah had some tough questions to ask.

The problem? No one wanted to answer her. And in all truth, maybe it was because no one had an answer. So week after week, Sarah came seeking, questioning, pleading for answers, and week after week she was sent home without any help.

"I just want to know the truth," she told her youth leader. "I just want to understand why God's Word can be trusted."

But instead of the leader offering to talk to her in private about her concerns, Sarah was told to just listen to the prescribed program and not ask so many questions.

The floor opened up, and Sarah quietly slipped through.

The bad thing is, no one noticed. Sarah stopped going to youth group and then church, and no one so much as called her to ask her why. It was as if they were all relieved to not be hearing her difficult questions anymore. Sarah turned to alcohol and drugs for her answers, finding friends who were more than happy to listen to her. Instead of hope in Jesus, Sarah quietly walked away from her Christian faith. After all, if the church couldn't give her answers, maybe the world could.

In both cases, needy, desperate people were lost to the church. They could have been productive. They could have grown spiritually. They could have influenced and helped others, but they fell through the cracks, and rather than tear up the floor or utilize a tool to get them back, the body of Christ decided they weren't worth the effort.

I heard the youth pastor proudly declare no more than a few weeks after Sarah's departure that their youth group was larger than ever, that the kids were growing in the Lord, and that several new arrivals had given their lives to Christ. Guess the hole in the floor got covered over with a rug.

A similar thing was true of Anna's situation. The church continued to grow, and two new Sunday school classes were formed: for divorcees and for young parents. Attendance numbers were up and giving was up. Anna wasn't missed. She was a sheep who had wandered off, and no shepherd cared enough to go after her.

Jesus told his disciples the parable of the lost sheep this way: "If a man owns a hundred sheep, and one of them wanders away, will he not leave the ninety-nine on the hills and go to look for the one that wandered off? And if he finds it, I tell you the truth, he is happier about that one sheep than about the ninety-nine that did not wander off. In the same way your Father in heaven is not willing that any of these little ones should be lost" (Matthew 18:12–14).

My son worked for over an hour to retrieve his little man. He was finally successful when his dad helped him come up with a useful tool: a coat hanger and a piece of chewed gum. Super sleuths and international spies, eat your hearts out.

Could the body of Christ not spend as much time and attention on retrieving those souls who have fallen through the cracks of the church? Is the effort required so great that no one is able to heed the call?

What kind of tool would it take to reach through the cracks and pull these people back in?

In Anna's case, it might have taken nothing more than a telephone call, a visit, or a note. Some evidence that someone cared.

And what of the Sarahs? Those teenagers who are asking difficult questions. Questions that strain the routine and tax the brains of leaders. Questions like "How do you know God really cares?" "If God loves me so much, then why does He allow bad things to happen to me?" "Does predestination mean that God planned for me to be this lonely?" "If I can't lose my salvation, then why should I worry about how I conduct myself?" or "If I can lose my salvation, how do I know when I've done something to lose it?"

The Sarahs of the world ask hard questions. They stare you straight in the face and rock the boat for answers. They pay little attention to proper church protocol, such as "Don't make the pastor/teacher/youth leader look stupid."

I know at least one Sarah very well. She's my older daughter, and she's still asking questions. She's come away from trying to answer those questions with the world's answers, but she still demands a lot out of her church body and spiritual leaders. She expects answers, and she wants those cracks in the floor fixed.

I want them fixed too. I want to be so concerned with the painful, desperate people that no one ever falls away unnoticed. I want to be an ambassador of Jesus Christ, who said that when the one is lost and the ninety-nine are sitting fat and sassy, I go after the one and find out where she slipped off to. I want to be a faithful example of His love and concern so that when those in the body ask hard questions, I can offer a listening ear and an answer. And if I don't have the answer, I want to care enough to seek out the answer.

I want to be a tool for Jesus. I want to be a coat hanger with chewed gum on the end so that I can reach down through the cracks and rescue the people who've fallen through. I want to be the person Jesus has called me to be. Real. Loving. Observant.

So clear the floor of the rugs and cover-ups. Look down those cracks—check those dark, lonely corners and hidden passageways. Send out search teams; rescue the fallen. The ninety-nine will still be there eating on the fat of the land when you bring back the one. The important thing is, bring back the one.

22

Disappointment

There's this guy I know, this editor fellow. He's neat and funny. Tells a good story, likes to hear a good story. He's zany and fun. He really did make a difference in my life, and it wouldn't be fair to write this book without mentioning him and what God taught me through him.

Steve is the kind of fellow you'd be pleased to know. He's just common folk—an everyday kind of Joe who wears an editor's cap for one of the nicest publishing establishments I know. He's also the very first editor I ever talked to face-to-face. Steve told me he wasn't looking for good books—he was looking for great books. And guess what? I had a good book—but not a great one. He quickly softened the blow by telling me that I was almost there, that I had talent, and I shouldn't give up.

Complimentary disappointment rained down like a summer shower.

I didn't want to hear that I was almost there. I wanted to hear that I *was* there. I wanted to so impress Steve that he would reach into his briefcase and pull out the "Author's Rich and Famous Contract" right there on the spot. I didn't want to have to go home and start over. I didn't want to try again.

Complimentary disappointment isn't any easier than regular disappointment. Face it. Disappointment is disappointment. It's that point in our lives where something we've strived for or sought after has been denied us. It's showing up an hour too late or being a dollar too short. It's being told *no* when your heart not only longs for *yes* but has actually counted on it.

The writing industry is full of disappointment. So is the rest of the world.

When I was in high school, we had tryouts for the spring musical. On a lark, my two girlfriends and I decided to give it a shot. We didn't want any solo parts; we only wanted to be in the chorus. One of us made it, and the other two didn't. It doesn't matter who was who, what mattered was the termination of our plans to experience this project together. All our dreams of attending rehearsals and eventually participating in the performance itself were over. The comment given to one of our trio was "Nice try. You've got a good voice, but it just isn't what we need for this musical."

Disappointment saturated us.

Sometimes this kind of disappointment is devastating. But other times it can be the best thing in the world.

Romans 5:3–5 says, "We also rejoice in our sufferings, because we know that suffering produces perseverance; perseverance, character; and character, hope. And hope does not disappoint us."

Sometimes we suffer disappointment for things that, while important to us, are not earth shattering. We face the rejection of a manuscript or a singing part. We don't get that job we've gone out after, or we lose the bid on a house we like. We're disappointed. But our suffering is minimal.

Other times the disappointment we face is monumental. We hear the words "I'm sorry, there's nothing more we can do." Or someone we care about says, "No, I won't forgive you."

Maybe you're facing one of those monumental types of disappointment. Maybe you've given your heart to God after years of poor judgments and sinful choices. Now you want the forgiveness of those you've wronged, but the answer is *no*. Maybe you've longed for a child of your own, and together you and your spouse have gone through all kinds of infertility treatments, only to be told that you'll never be able to have a baby.

The pain is very real whether it comes in monumental sizes or in complimentary disappointments. Our hearts hurt for the rejection or the loss.

God's Word says that these sufferings should give us cause to rejoice. Excuse me? I'm supposed to be happy that there's no cure for the cancer that is killing my loved one? I'm supposed to smile and give a great big "Thank you!" when someone refuses to let me participate in my heart's dreams and desires?

Oh, this is a hard one. Rejoicing in suffering, no matter the degree to which we suffer, is not something that comes naturally. Neither is it exactly what I think we've often been led to believe. Does God really expect us to dance a jig of joy when we get bad news? I don't think so.

Isaiah 66:13 says, "As a mother comforts her child, so will I [the Lord] comfort you."

If God is offering comfort, it can't be a sin for us to seek comfort. When our hearts are broken or even disappointed, God allows us to crawl up onto His lap and have a good cry. He's there to comfort and encourage us back to the place where we can go on.

I think the verse in Romans speaks to our seeing the opportunity for a closer walk with Jesus—for a chance to improve, and for God to take us in a different direction. So often the direction and plans we have for ourselves fall so far short of what God has in mind for us that He has to put a roadblock up in order to keep us from going down the wrong road. Sometimes the path He sends us on is a labor for us to endure, but it's a labor well worth the outcome.

Romans says, "Suffering produces perseverance."

My mother used to say that perseverance was another word for "stick-to-itiveness." It's that "If at first you don't succeed . . ." saying. The sorrow over my complimentary disappointment with my editor caused me to go back to the drawing board. I attended additional writing workshops. I honed my skills and went to work to find my voice.

"Perseverance [produces] character."

In working to develop my writing, God also went to work to develop my character. My immaturity began to fade a bit as my spirit grew in a closer walk with Him. My stubbornness, intolerance, and complete lack of patience underwent a work-over. A more positive character emerged. Oh, there's still a lot of work to be done, believe me, but character development moved me to the next phase. Hope.

"Character [produces] hope, and hope does not disappoint us."

Hope. What a beautiful word. The anticipation of something positive. The expectation that good is coming just over the next hill.

My character developed, and as perseverance and God continued to work me through the suffering, hope jumped in from out of nowhere (it seemed) and joined me on the journey. Where suffering had robbed me of energy, hope bolstered me. Where perseverance had wearied me, hope gave me strength. Where character came about only through growing pains, hope lovingly tended the wounds and supported me on my way.

Hope is a marvelous thing to have. Hope does not disappoint us. Not in a complimentary way or in a heartless way. Hope promises that the best is yet to come. It says not only are you on the right path but you've nearly finished the race!

Maybe you're sitting here reading this right now and hope is the one thing that you know is missing in your life. It's been gone so long you aren't even sure what it looks like anymore. Suffering has buckled your knees and stripped you of every resource. Not only is the light at the end of the tunnel missing but you aren't even sure where the tunnel is.

Rejoice. Not in yourself. Not in your own strength. But since your knees are buckled anyway, why not try a bit of prayer? Open your heart, even if it's broken and bleeding. Start with something simple.

"God, you are the only one who cares."

God is steadfast. Rejoice.

"God, I don't know where to go from here, but you do."

God is all-knowing. Rejoice.

"God, I can't do this alone."

God is faithful. Rejoice.

"God, I hurt so bad."

God is the great healer. Rejoice.

Suffering gives way in prayer and hope is born. And hope does not disappoint us. Why? Go back to Romans 5:5 and pick up the rest of the verse.

"And hope does not disappoint us, because God has poured His love into our hearts by the Holy Spirit, whom He has given us."

The editor told me my writing was "almost there." God tells us He's "already here." He's poured out his love and hope, and He won't disappoint us.

Life gives us no easy answers. No simple plans. We have disappointments to face and trials to overcome. We will suffer—Jesus told us we would. We will go without and lose people we care about and things we enjoyed. We will be told "No!" And, we will get our feelings hurt. But don't let disappointment have the final word. Don't let suffering rob you of what is rightfully yours.

Perseverance—character—hope.

"And hope does not disappoint us."

23

Our Duty

O nce upon a time, there was a man who sat in prison awaiting his execution. Every day he hoped and prayed he'd be pardoned—reprieved. The day of his execution neared, and still there was no sign of the governor's releasing him.

Miles away in the state capitol, the governor looked at the request for pardon. He took pity on the man and issued forgiveness. The man was to be spared the death sentence and instead would serve out his days in prison. The governor handed over his decision to a clerk and asked that the man deliver the good news.

The clerk, however, wasn't all that concerned with what he had to convey. On his way to the prison, he dropped off his dry cleaning, made a stop at the bank, argued with a gas station attendant who informed him that there were no longer any full-service pumps, and finally stopped to get himself something from the local burger joint.

He showed up at the prison to deliver the letter at the same hour the man was to be executed. He went to see the warden, but didn't identify himself or his business. As he sat waiting to see the warden, he sucked down the last of his soda from the fast-food restaurant and mentally planned his evening. When the warden finally showed up and asked the man his business, the man handed over the governor's letter and proceeded to walk away.

"Wait!" the warden cried, "I have just put this man to death. What am I supposed to do with this news?"

The man turned and shrugged. "That's not my problem. I brought the news. What you do with it is up to you."

Then there is the story of the surgeon who stood over his patient. The sick man writhed in pain and pleaded for the doctor's help. "You'll only get out of this what you choose to," the surgeon told him.

The man, quite stunned, questioned the doctor. "What do you mean? I'm in pain and I need help. I can hardly fix myself. You are the one with the knowledge to save my life, but you're telling me that I'll only get out of it what I choose to get out of it? What is that supposed to mean?"

The surgeon shook his head. "It means exactly that. It's true, I've come to this room with the knowledge needed to ease your pain, but it's up to you to receive it in a proper manner."

The doctor's answer completely baffled the man and did nothing to ease his misery.

Often we deal with situations and people who are on the brink of death, particularly spiritual death, or writhing in pain from their own sins or the suffering inflicted upon them through the sins of others. We deliver the Word of God, giving wonderful platitudes of faith. We preach from pulpits, dictate the law from the front of a classroom, and then walk away from the situation feeling that we've done our duty. We delivered the news. We brought the knowledge needed. Our part of the task is finished. It's up to those hurting, dying people to be benefited by our mission.

This is a falsehood that has done more to cripple than any other I know. We somehow get in our heads that our responsibility—our duty—is a very limited one. We hear sermons on how we sow the seeds but may never reap the harvest. And while that's true, it doesn't mean it's set in stone—that this is how it will be every time. We may well sow seeds *and* harvest those fields. We may deliver the Good News and find ourselves needing to go beyond platitudes and sermons to something practical. We may be asked to give something more, and find that in doing so, we will also need to continue to give . . . and to give . . . and to give.

In Matthew 5:41 Jesus says, "If someone forces you to go one mile, go with him two miles." Jesus also said that we have to deny self and take up our cross daily and follow Him. Sometimes going the extra mile with someone requires that we deny self. And sometimes that's not exactly what we want to do.

When my husband was in college, he had a professor who openly confessed pride in his fail rate. He told his class that he had the highest failing rate in the entire college. He took this as a badge of honor. He thought it meant that his subject was so difficult, the knowledge so lofty and unattainable, that unless the student really applied himself, really sunk his teeth into the meat of the topic and gave it his all, he would fail the course.

It apparently never occurred to the professor that the problem might be that his teaching techniques were less than effective or that his style was antiquated and that he had no heart for his students.

As brothers and sisters in the Lord, we are called upon to nurture and encourage one another. It is our duty to bear one another's burdens. To feed the sheep. I once heard from the pulpit that it wasn't the pastor's job to feed the congregation; his job was to preach to the unsaved so that they might accept salvation. It was the responsibility of those already saved to find food for themselves. I have a problem with this. Not that I don't believe we have certain responsibilities to continue our growth in Jesus Christ. After all, that's what this book is all about.

What I have a problem with is that sometimes people—good people, honest people, saved people, are struggling in the daily grind just to draw their next breath. And if breathing is a task, then how can we in leadership roles expect them to feed themselves?

What about those in need of critical care—those too wounded and sick to get off their sick beds and walk to the cupboard? What about those whose sickness affects their minds, and they don't know how to care for themselves anymore? What about those who are too exhausted to move? They'd honestly like to dig into a platter of spiritual meat, but they haven't got the energy to figure out where they can find such a meal.

Jesus told Peter on three different occasions in the twenty-first chapter of John to feed His lambs, take care of His sheep, and to feed His sheep. He gave Peter a duty—the same duty He gives us.

Sheep rely on the shepherd to take them to pasture. They need his guidance and direction. They can't very well walk to the fridge for a snack, nor can a lamb prepare its own bottle of milk. They need help to find food. They need to be led in order to be fed.

Christians of all spiritual ages and walks need to be fed as well. Jesus wasn't talking about the beasts in the field when he instructed Peter. He was talking about the sheep in his spiritual flock. He wanted Peter to provide spiritual food to feed the lambs and sheep of Jesus' kingdom. Jesus calls us to feed one another as well. To offer nourishment in times of hunger. To keep the hungry from starving to death.

When the people flocked to Jesus with their hearts sincerely seeking, Jesus shared living water and the bread of life. He didn't ask them first to prove they were worthy. He didn't tell them that they should go out there and find their own food. He didn't tell them they'd only get out of it what they chose to, and He didn't throw the Good News at them, leaving them confused and uncertain, and then tell them what they did with it was up to them.

The Canaanite woman pleaded with Jesus, "Lord, Son of David, have mercy on me!" Her daughter was demon possessed, and she wanted Jesus to help. The account in Matthew 15 says that Jesus didn't answer her, so His disciples came to Him and urged Him to send her away. She was a nuisance; she was disturbing their peace with her neediness. Ever see that in the church today?

Jesus tells them, "I was sent only to the lost sheep of Israel." The woman in turn begs Him for help again. Jesus then replies, "It is not right to take the children's bread and toss it to their dogs."

"Yes, Lord," she said, "but even the dogs eat the crumbs that fall from their masters' table" (vv. 22–27).

Jesus praised her for her faith and healed her daughter. Jesus saw her hunger—her need. He sees our hunger and need as well. He hears our heart's questions even when the world, including the church, chooses to ignore them. He didn't require anything more of her than the fact that she had come in faith—in her neediness. He didn't reject her because she needed more of Him than He was ready to give. After all, He tells her that He's come for the lost sheep of Israel, and she doesn't fit the bill. But even though this woman had a need that was outside the realm of everyone's expectation and plan, Jesus blessed her and healed her daughter.

Can we as ambassadors of Christ do any less? Will we stand by the side of the road and smile at the passing hungry masses? Will we tell them to find their own food, to feed themselves? Will we stand in our loftiness with knowledge and understanding and refuse to share what we have? Will we deny our duty?

Jesus says, "Come, you who are blessed by my Father, take your inheritance, the kingdom prepared for you since the creation of the world. For I was hungry and you gave me something to eat" (Matthew 25:34–35).

There are hungry sheep to be fed.

There are starving baby lambs that need a bottle of milk.

You may be the only one who has the opportunity to feed them. Don't send them away hungry. Don't leave them to their own care.

Listen to the Master—He's calling to you now.

"Feed my sheep. Feed my lambs. Feed my people."

24

Causes and the Cross

In this day and age, we are absolutely inundated with causes of every kind. There are causes to help those who are sick, causes to help animals, causes to help workers, and causes to help causes. My children actually came out of grade school knowing more about causes than about the things I considered necessary to their education.

We love our causes. Causes give us purpose and direction. We find something we truly believe in and go after it with great gumption. Maybe it's as simple as becoming a worker in an organization we believe in. Maybe it's more involved and takes us on multiple journeys around the world. You can take up political causes, religious causes, and educational causes. People give hours and hours of time to one cause or another. They work at raising money, raising awareness, and raising indignation.

There's no end of causes in the United States. Even a diet or exercise plan can become a cause, taking our focus and time in a regular routine of events.

Religious organizations are probably some of the biggest cause-focused groups. We find ourselves participating in the choir, the women's ministry, the community food shelf, and children's church. We busy ourselves in the service of God, but sometimes lose sight of God himself.

Now, don't get me wrong. I believe in service and causes. Christian radio has been one of my favorites. I met a really neat friend through Christian radio—a man with a real heart for God. His participation and love of the ministry of Christian radio opened my eyes to a whole new mission field. Christian publishing is another cause that I'm obviously behind and supportive of. Crisis pregnancy centers, supporting pro-life, have rated high in my book, as have causes dealing with helping the illiterate, veterans, the homeless, and just about anything to do with children.

But first and foremost, all causes aside, I believe in the cross of Jesus Christ. Jesus didn't espouse causes. He espoused obedience to the Father. And in that obedience, He met the needs of His people. He didn't act out of pride or forced allegiance. He didn't come forward because it was expected of Him. He didn't step out because the synagogue would look down upon Him if He didn't. He came in obedience, and He went to the cross in obedience.

Oswald Chambers, one of my very favorite writers, says this in his classic devotional *My Utmost for His Highest*:

> Today we have substituted credal beliefs for personal belief,
> and that is why so many are devoted to causes and so few

devoted to Jesus Christ. People do not want to be devoted to Jesus, but only to the cause He started. Jesus Christ is a source of deep offense to the educated mind of today that does not want Him in any other way than as a Comrade.[2]

Or as we like to call it in our house, "the fluffy bunny Jesus" syndrome.

The cause Jesus started is frightening to us, and so thinking of Jesus as a soft-hearted, fluffy God—the kind of buddy or pal who would overlook the wrong we do with a smile and say, "Oh well, I still love you, ya big lug," is much easier to contend with.

Jesus came out of obedience, and obedience terrifies us. Obedience was hard for us as children. I remember one of our daughters getting caught red-handed in something she knew better than to be doing. Her response was something like "I really wanted to mind you." The spirit was willing, but the flesh was weak.

It really gets no easier as adults. We want to obey the speed limit, but we're going to be late to work unless we push past that limit. Then we're angry and frustrated when we catch sight of the flashing red lights in the rearview mirror. And we blame the cop for our indiscretion.

Causes are easy, but obedience is hard. Unless we yield first to Jesus. Even then, as human beings we are going to struggle with our choices. Causes almost seem simple compared to obedience. We bury ourselves in the pretense of obedience by giving of our time and efforts in order to avoid the real issue: a prideful, unbroken spirit, a willful heart that demands control or glory or self-gratification. Sometimes the real cause we seek to serve is self.

Several years ago I heard a man say that he highly regarded and supported the cause of Mother Teresa, that dear little dynamo of missions, who worked with the lowest of the lowly in India. I thought to myself at the time that had Mother Teresa heard his statement, it would have grieved her to the core of her heart. She wasn't into her own cause. It wasn't Mother Teresa's cause at all, but rather the cause of obedience to God. God had called her to work for Him. God gave her a mission field with many unique problems and needs. God even brought her into a work that needed champions to help support and fund it, creating it into a type of cause. But it was God's cause—it was a cause of love and obedience. I'm fully convinced that if Mother Teresa could have gone about the earth working for God in complete secret, she would have done exactly that. She wasn't working for fame or fortune. She was showing her love for God in the one way she knew best. Obedience.

On the flip side of that coin was Princess Diana. Here too was a woman who was called to various missions. She had cause after cause that made the front page of every paper in the world. She worked with AIDS patients. She worked to eliminate land mines. She worked to support so many charities that she needed several secretaries just to keep everything straight. Her very public status made her the perfect focal figure for these organizations. Those in charge knew that wherever she went, the press and people would follow, and this, they hoped, would result in additional funding, charitable contributions, and maybe even volunteers for their organizations.

Diana's heart may well have been in the right place. She may very well have loved and adored helping the sick and injured. I cannot say that she didn't have a heart of love and compassion. But because of who she was to the people around her, the focus was always Diana. She may not have wanted it that way, but by the very nature of the situation, that's the way it was.

Two very different women. A multitude of various causes. But one did her deeds out of obedience to the Lord. She wanted no glory for herself. She only wanted to be God's ambassador of love to a dying and hopeless world.

These two women died within a week of each other. I might not have even known about Mother Teresa's death except for hearing about it at church. Because of the volatile and unexpected nature of Princess Diana's death in a car accident, and because of who she was and what she represented to the world—beauty, youth, popularity, money, power—she was all we heard about on the news for weeks.

Mother Teresa slipped quietly into the arms of Jesus, no doubt hearing, "Well done, my good and faithful servant." I know Mother Teresa would probably have had it no other way. She wouldn't have wanted the world's glory heaped upon her deeds. She wouldn't want them espousing the "cause of Mother Teresa," because that would take the focus away from the God she so dearly loved and served.

The focus of our attention must never be the cause. Because no matter what cause you choose or how noble the issue, the cause of Jesus must overshadow it or it's nothing more than clanging cymbals. The cause of Jesus was obedience to the Father. The result of that cause was an outpouring of love so wondrous and rich that it led Jesus to the cross of Calvary. And the love that poured down from the cross is the same love that leads us home.

Are you weary of the causes in your life? Did you seek to fulfill yourself in deeds and showy routines, only to find there was nothing there to satisfy the longing of your heart? Are you in the business of busyness, yet have an empty place in your heart that refuses to be filled?

I know who can fill that emptiness.

Mother Teresa knew who could fill it as well.

Only Jesus satisfies. Jesus is the only cause you need. In loving and obeying Him, you'll find the direction He would have you go. You'll find those purposes and deeds that need to be performed. But better yet, you'll find Him in a most intimate and personal way—a way that will lead you home.

25

As a Little Child

At my son's first Christmas, we gifted him with a stuffed animal that he was to later dub "Kitty." The only "problem," and it never really was that much of a problem, was that this was a stuffed bear and not a cat.

The bear was fluffy and full faced, however, and my son was convinced that this was a kitty. Kitty soon became a vested member of the family. He and my son, Erik, shared the strangest relationship of love that I've ever witnessed between a child and a toy.

When Erik would be upset and crying, he would pause in mid-cry to cry for Kitty. We witnessed this in disbelief the first couple of times. Erik would cry, tears streaming down his face. Then Kitty would cry, Erik holding him up, saying, "Mew, mew, mew."

Kitty became a companion extraordinaire. Kitty traveled when Erik traveled. If Erik went to Grandma and Grandpa's house, Kitty went there as well. If Erik went to the zoo, Kitty went to the zoo.

Kitty has traveled to more states (even one foreign country) than most people I know. I don't want to tell you how many frequent-flyer miles Kitty has logged, but let's just say he can go first-class to Europe anytime he wants.

Kitty started out fluffy and clean, all gray and white with a sweet, contented, Buddha-like smile on his face. He was stuffed full and sat up by himself in regal form. Twelve years later, however, he's had the stuffing loved right out of him. His fur has been loved off, and he's undergone many rounds of plastic surgery.

One such surgery came as a result of my son's having taken Kitty to spend the night with some family friends. Erik hadn't experienced overnights on his own before, so he took Kitty with him. After all, if you're going to be in a strange place, it's best to have a friend along. We warned him that something could happen to Kitty. He could get misplaced or damaged, but our son wouldn't take no for answer. If Kitty couldn't go, he wouldn't go.

What neither Kitty nor my son expected was Dumplin'. Dumplin' is a sweetheart of a golden retriever. Generally mild-mannered and a friend to all, nobody thought anything about Dumplin' and Kitty spending time together. But as is often the case, tragedy came in the unexpected.

I was on my way to bed when the phone call came. A very subdued little boy spoke to me from the other end of the line. "Mom?" he said, his voice slightly quivering. "There's been an accident."

Of course, my mind ran rampant. Had he broken his arm? Cut his foot? Was it some other type of accident—you know, the embarrassing bathroom kind?

"What's happened?" I asked, trying my best to keep my voice from sounding too anxious.

"Dumplin' chewed off Kitty's nose." His voice broke, but he recovered quickly. "Mom, come get us."

My friend came on the line about that time and explained that Kitty and Dumplin' had been left alone to share amiable company, when they apparently had some sort of disagreement. We believe it might have been theological or political, but, of course, we can't prove it. The disagreement resulted in Dumplin's chewing off not only the nose but a good portion of the face. Stuffing was pouring out, and the nose was missing.

My heart went out to my son. I knew what he was feeling. He was shocked and mortified that this had happened, but he was also heartbroken because his best friend was wounded.

"You don't have to come get him," my friend said. "After all, it is after midnight."

"No, that's all right," I replied, knowing that my son would never sleep a wink so long as Kitty was in misery.

I left my daughters and husband at home and set out on the rescue mission. As I drove across town, I tried to think of how I would deal with the situation. I didn't want to baby my son too much. It was bad enough that I was giving in to getting him in the middle of the night. I knew the psychologists would probably never agree with my actions, but I didn't care. I heard the brokenness in my little boy's voice. I had to be there for him, to prove that I was never more than a phone call away.

When I arrived at my friend's house, the place was in mild chaos. The boys all met me at the door. Erik fought hard to keep from crying as he hugged me close and held up the plastic-wrapped bundle.

"He's . . . in here," Erik whispered stoically.

"Erik said you would fix Kitty tonight," one of the boys said.

Another one chimed in, "But we told him you wouldn't 'cause it's so late, and Kitty is so torn up."

My son looked to me, his expression full of faith. "I told them you could fix Kitty," Erik said, as if to answer all their doubts. "I told them you knew it was important, and you would do it for me."

There is nothing in this world that would have kept me from fixing that poor ragged bear for my son. His faith in me was overwhelming. I could have broken both arms on the way back home, and still I would have found a way to stitch Kitty back together. I wanted very much for my son to believe—to have faith—in my love for him.

We turned to go, and my girlfriend apologized. "Oh, by the way, we couldn't find Kitty's nose."

I nodded, seeing the impossibility of it all. I don't think I have ever prayed harder for the skills of a surgeon than I did that night. Once we were in the car, my son broke into tears and leaned against me, heartbroken.

"I hate that dog!" he sobbed.

"No, don't hate Dumplin'," I said. "She's just a dog, and she didn't know any better. She didn't do this to be mean to Kitty or to you."

Erik calmed down a bit. "You will fix Kitty, won't you?"

I heard the need for reassurance in his voice. "I'll do what I can."

"And you'll do it when we get home?"

"Absolutely," I promised.

Erik leaned back and nodded. He wiped his tears away. "I told them you would."

I don't know about you, but I want that kind of faith. I want to bring my broken toys to God and know without the slightest hint of doubt that He will fix them. I want to be able to say with as much confidence as a small boy that my Father would take care of the matter—and take care of it in a manner that would befit my need.

In Mark 10:14–15, Jesus is rather indignant with his disciples. People are bringing their children to him for a blessing—a touch, but the disciples see this as a nuisance. Jesus tells them, "Let the little children come to me, and do not hinder them, for the kingdom of God belongs to such as these. I tell you the truth, anyone who will not receive the kingdom of God like a little child will never enter it."

These verses bless my heart. Maybe it's because I always feel rather childlike and intimidated by great theological minds with multiple initials following their names. Maybe it's because I've always known that God is the Creator of the universe, but I've never cared about how He did it beyond His speaking it into existence. And maybe it's because when I'm faced with difficult situations, I go running to the lap of my heavenly Father first, and that's where I want to stay.

My heart often feels very much like a child's heart. The new and wondrous things of this earth easily excite me. And I trust my Father in heaven to provide what I need, when I need it, before I even know I need it.

Does this mean I've never had any doubts? Certainly not! Does it mean that I've never questioned God about bad situations? Nope. Does it mean that I'm always in right accordance with my Father because of some great faith within me? Absolutely not!

It simply means that after years and years of taking my needs to God, He has never failed to stay up late enough to fix them. He's never denied me in front of my friends. He's never turned away, saying, "Well, you knew there was a possibility of this happening; now deal with it on your own."

So how do we receive the kingdom of God like a little child?

As I stitched on Kitty's broken face, with tiny dedicated stitches, I couldn't help but think of God and how His love for me was even greater than my love for Erik. How He desires to heal our wounds, comfort us in times of pain, and fix the wrongs. I wanted to display my trust in God with the same overwhelming confidence that my son had displayed trust in me.

I finished Kitty's surgery with a tremendous sense of accomplishment. He was a little worse for the wear, but not much. He was still smiling with his renewed simplistic smile, and he now had a new nose, brown instead of black. But most important, he was still Kitty.

Erik had waited for me in the living room, and when I entered the room, I felt like a doctor exiting surgery. And truly, that's what I was. Erik looked up at me with no less hope than that of a parent awaiting word on his injured child.

I held up Kitty.

Erik smiled and took his worn bear in hand. "Thanks, Mom," he said, hugging me tight. "I knew you could do it."

The look on his face said it all. The trust was evident. There was no room for a single thread of doubt.

O God, I want the faith of an eight-year-old.

26

The Pain of Rejection

O ne of the most heartbreaking pains in the world is to be rejected by someone you love. Especially when it's someone who should have loved you. The pain is like a dull ache that refuses to be stilled. There's an emptiness that seems bottomless, a canyon that seems to widen and grow ever deeper as the years go by. That's the pain of being rejected by someone who should have loved you—someone who should have cared.

In America, we see the tragedy of this rejection in such great proportions. Daily thousands, hundreds of thousands, of children awaken to the fact of life without one or both parents. They must face the cold, hard truth that someone who should have loved them, who should have cared enough to be a part of their lives, isn't there anymore.

We wonder why so many teenagers become delinquent. Why teenagers turn to sexual love at such an early age. We see children killing children. We hear the sorrow of their hearts in the deadliness of their actions.

When I was two and a half years old, my mother and father were divorced. It was one of those unavoidable tragedies that we see every day in life. There were good reasons for the breakup of this family. There were even biblical reasons. But it wasn't desired, and it wasn't pleasant.

Sometime later my mother remarried a wonderful, kindhearted man. He was a good stepfather. In fact, he is the only father I remember. However, he could never fill the emptiness of the place left by my biological father.

There was a place in my heart that had been ripped away. My stepfather tried to fill that empty place. He worked hard to provide for my mother and me. He drove us to church every Sunday. He was affectionate and fun loving. He was everything a father should be. He was everything my biological father refused to be. The most important thing was that my stepfather was there for me. He stayed and didn't go away into some void where people are X'd out of your life.

I know at least a dozen friends and family members who can relate the same story. Oh, the pain that has flooded their hearts. That ripped-out place was never filled—it simply scarred over. In some cases, it festered and became infected until the whole body was poisoned and affected.

Sometimes the scar has faded with time. Like with my experience. Having a family, a loving stepfather and mother, and a new baby sister, my wound healed to some extent, and the scar faded over the years. But sometimes I still wonder why. Why did my biological father leave my life and never come back? Why didn't he care enough to get his act together and be a real father to me? Why did he forsake me?

I used to think how this problem is unique to mankind. I thought it was a problem God could not entirely understand. After all, God is the great I Am. He has always been and will always be. How could He know what it felt like to be deserted—forsaken by the one person who should never have left your side?

Then I thought of Jesus on the cross. I thought of His pain and misery. He was beaten, scorned, rejected, and delivered into the hands of people who didn't care what happened to Him. He was just one more crazy lunatic in a long line of religious and political fanatics.

But He still had His Father in heaven. He still had the Holy Spirit to comfort Him in His hour of need. He walked the road to the cross, still in the company of the only one who would never die—never walk away—never leave Him.

But on the cross, bearing the sins of the world, bearing my sin and yours, Jesus came to that horrible, awful place where God seemed distant. When I was young, my Sunday school teacher said that God could not look upon sin, and Jesus was, at that point, like a very big, ugly ball of sin. When I was in an adult Sunday school class, the pastor said that Jesus, being the very essence of God in human form, was an abomination to himself.

God looked away.

Jesus cried out, "My God, my God, why have you forsaken me?"

Those words are so precious to me. Jesus knew. He really knew what it felt like to have His Father turn away. He knows what it feels like to have someone who has cared before—who should be there for every single pain and tear—no longer be there.

But God wasn't absent for long, and Jesus knew it was all a part of the plan. How else could He be our High Priest—to know the deepest sorrows of our hearts, and to fill the emptiness?

Jesus is also the only one who will ever fill the empty places created by people. Jesus is the only one who knows how very frightening it can be to feel abandoned.

Maybe you have an empty place in your heart. Perhaps your mother or father walked away and never came back. It could have been by his or her choice, or maybe he or she died. In any case, it still feels like abandonment. It still hurts.

That empty place was never filled—partly because you always kept hoping against all odds that it was somehow a mistake, and partly because you wanted to believe your parent would come back.

Maybe a close friend has decided to end your friendship. You haven't got a clue as to why she no longer wants to be friends—you only have the emptiness felt by her having gone.

Jesus can fill that vacuum. He can take away the longing in your soul, the rejection you feel. Jesus is the only one who will never in a million gazillion years walk away.

Why?

Because He knows how it feels. Because He loves you with an unconditional love and has promised never to leave you or forsake you, and because you belong to Him.

"But what if I sin? What if I do something horrible?" you may ask.

He'll still love you. He'll still be there.

"But what if I forget to pray or read my Bible?"

He still loves you. He's still there.

"But what if I walk away?"

No problem. He still loves you.

Does He want you to sin or forget to pray or to walk away? No. He doesn't want to break communion with you for even a brief moment. Because He loves you and He wants to spend time with you.

But if you walk away, He'll still be there. He'll stand faithfully watching for you—calling to you. "Come home, beloved. Come home."

You can never outdistance yourself from Jesus. You can never hide away so completely that He cannot find you.

Do you have an empty place inside that needs to be filled? Is there a spot that aches so horribly that nothing—drugs, money, people—can fill it?

Come home, beloved. Jesus is waiting to pour himself into that empty place. He wants to fill you so completely that all the little spots, as well as the big ones, are no longer empty, but instead radiate the light of His love.

People will die or forsake you. Possessions will fall apart and fade away. But Jesus is forever.

Let Jesus fill you up.

27

Great Expectations

E xpectations come in two packages: the good kind and the bad kind. When I was four months along in my third pregnancy, I held great expectations for the outcome. We were excited about the baby—hopeful it would be a boy, but happy to take whatever God chose so long as he or she was healthy.

Like many expectant mothers, I anticipated the birth of my child with great wonder and awe. The miracle of birth, the joy of God's hand upon this small life growing inside of me, all of those incredible moments from the first heartbeat to the first kick—it was amazing and wonderful.

Then everything changed.

"Your blood tests show that something is wrong," the doctor told me.

The foundations of my expectations were shattered and lay in ruins all around me. Tests suggested a serious problem with the baby—problems that would result in severe retardation and death.

"My suggestion is that you abort this pregnancy," one doctor stated matter-of-factly. "You're young and healthy and can certainly have more children. Why saddle your family with a child who will only cause you grief and pain?"

I was devastated. I wanted this baby, anticipated this baby with the same joy and wonder that I had my first two children. But in the doctor's few words, my great expectations of joy were transferred to expectations of dread and worry.

I would like to say that I handled the matter in a peaceful, angelic sort of spirit. I did not. I was angry and hurt and scared. I didn't believe in abortion. No matter what the result, I knew I could not end my child's life. I felt strongly that life and death were choices better left up to God. Like Job, I wanted to stand strong and say, "Though you slay me, yet will I trust you." Because I really did trust God. I might not have understood, but I did trust Him.

Trusting didn't make the situation any easier; in fact, it made it harder. I longed for a quick and simple solution. Abortion certainly wasn't the answer. Even if I had seen it as an option, I've never believed that abortion was anyone's "easy way out." I know women who've had abortions. There was nothing easy about it.

My expectation upon learning I was pregnant was that this pregnancy would go as smoothly and simply as any pregnancy could. That was what I had prepared myself for—what I had planned for. Problems were not factored in, because I held the utmost optimism that nothing could or would go wrong. Those things happened to other people, not to me.

There's something about becoming cocky and self-sufficient

that always sets us up for a life lesson. This was one of my life lessons, and let me tell you, it was the painful kind.

I thought every day about that baby and how very much I wanted him or her to be born healthy and whole. I railed at God . . . demanding answers . . . pleading for understanding . . . begging for the life of my child. I remember specifically telling God that He couldn't convince me that anything good could come out of this situation—this time of testing and trial.

I was hurt. I was angry. I was terrified.

Because I refused to abort the baby, the doctors classified this as a high-risk pregnancy. I was required to come for checkups more often and was constantly watched for any little problem. In the meantime, Christmas was nearly upon us, and I began to pray like I'd never prayed before.

My expectations were shot. Now all I wanted was the peace that passes understanding. Now all I needed was God's healing touch, His gentle hand, His loving reassurance that He would see me through.

I heard the words from Isaiah, "For unto us a child is born, unto us a son is given . . ." (9:6 KJV).

I wanted so much for those words to be true for our family, and as I prayed, God worked a miracle in my heart. The peace did come, the anticipation of God's promise to be there for me—to hold me and keep me—gave me strength. I felt the peace I so longed to know, and the expectation that was born was one of knowing that no matter what lay at the end of the road, God would take every step with me; I would never be alone. He didn't take away the problem, but He assured me of my safety, of His guardianship.

As the pregnancy drew to an end, we had already endured many problems. I developed pneumonia during the middle trimester and had to be put on complete bed rest. I missed a lot of work and then had to go to half days. My employer wasn't happy about it, commenting behind my back that this was a lot of trouble and effort for a baby who was going to die anyway.

As I woke up on Mother's Day, 1989, I felt mildly uncomfortable and knew my labor had started. I couldn't help but turn to God in prayer. What would happen this day? Mother's Day, of all days.

Our expectations were so very different than they had been in the beginning. My husband and I had thought we'd known how things would go. I had figured it all out very carefully and had detailed all my plans. Now, preparing to deliver this baby, nothing but God remained a sure thing.

As my labor increased, I felt the peace of God engulf me. My husband, Jim, had told me a few months earlier that God had given him assurance that all would be well. I clung to that assurance. No matter the outcome.

I also clung to the expectation that all of this had come about for a reason. Remember, I'm the one who told God that no good could come out of this. Well, God would prove me wrong on that measure, and He would do so in a spectacular manner. But I'm getting ahead of myself.

Erik was born shortly before eight o'clock that evening. He was perfectly whole and wonderfully healthy. A lovely, beautiful baby boy was added to our family.

I wanted to sing and shout and dance before the Lord. I wanted to hold my son up as evidence to the medical world that they didn't know best—God did. I wanted to write a letter to every abortion supporter, tack a picture of my son at the top, and tell them what choice was really all about.

Several years later I would write about this experience for a small Sunday school take-home paper. The story ran on Mother's Day—my son's birthday. To my surprise, and extreme blessing, an editor friend sent me a note some time after that. She'd received a story of hope and joy for the magazine she was working with. The story was about a woman who had found herself in my situation. She had been told to abort her unborn child because of problems that showed up on tests. She was in turmoil over what to do when she read my story about Erik. She decided then and there to trust God and let Him lead her through the situation. Her child was born some months later. The baby needed a few minor medical helps, but was otherwise healthy. I cried and cried over that letter.

I had told God that nothing good could come out of my situation. I had been confident that nothing positive, productive, or otherwise beneficial could possibly come about out of a troubled pregnancy. I was wrong.

Expectations are funny things. We find ourselves elated and excited by some, disappointed and sorrowed by others.

Romans 8:19 states, "The creation waits in eager expectation for the sons of God to be revealed." The return of Jesus, the new heaven and new earth, a life with no more tears, are things that some people look forward to with great expectation. They long for heaven and the end of this world so that all things might be in perfect order, and Satan might be completely and permanently defeated.

Others are less than enthusiastic, however. Their expectation is one of dread. "If we deliberately keep on sinning after we have received the knowledge of the truth, no sacrifice for sins is left, but only a fearful expectation of judgment and of raging fire that will consume the enemies of God" (Hebrews 10:26–27).

Doctors say that stress can kill. Stress can be a fearful expectation: the dread that hangs over you like the sword of Damocles—growing ever closer, threatening to end your life. Fearful expectation is knowing things are headed in the wrong direction. Often this fearfulness is born out of sin: you've made the wrong choice or you've fallen short of what you were supposed to do, choosing instead to ignore the truth. In this case, fearful expectation is the undeniable realization that there will be consequences to suffer if you don't change your ways.

Maybe you find yourself in that state of mind today. You know there's something you should do, but you've avoided it—put it off—buried it as deep as you can. You've wounded a friend and need to seek his forgiveness. You've falsely judged someone and gossiped about her behind her back. You've chosen circumstantial evidence instead of learning the facts. The dread washes over you in waves, staining you with each touch. Fearful expectation is eating you alive.

When I lied to my mother about whether I'd cleaned my room, when I sinned against God knowing that I should choose another path, I felt that overwhelming fearful expectation.

If you know this feeling, if you're swallowed whole by that dread sensation of fearful expectation, then I encourage you to figure out what's at the center of that feeling. Something's gone undone. Someone is hurt and you're to blame.

My mother used to say, "The only time it's too late to change what you've done or haven't done is when you're dead." It's not too late to make the past right. It's not too late to mend those relationships or ask forgiveness for those wrongs. It's only too late if you're dead.

Are you tired of that fearfulness, that sense of darkness and horror? Do you feel like God is waiting on the sidelines with some God-sized flyswatter, just hoping to catch you unaware and punish you for what you've done? Have you exhausted yourself running from what you know has to be done—what you know, painfully and clearly, can only be done by you?

Expectations need not be of a fearful nature. Imagine for yourself a clean slate, a fresh start, a forgiven heart. What's causing that fearfulness? Close your eyes and see the burden you're carrying. Unbury it and look at it for what it is—a mechanism Satan uses to separate us from God. Lay it at God's feet and let it go. Ask forgiveness, smooth out the rough spots. The price is relatively inexpensive compared to the destructive cost of leaving it untended.

God has a way of bringing us to those places where He alone can turn the fearful expectation into great expectations of joy and hope.

The choice is up to us. What will you choose?

As he steps into his teen years, my son is a joy and delight to our family. He also has his moments of causing us discomfort and concern, but the point is, he's alive and well, able to be anything he likes. I have great expectations for this child, and all of them are steeped in the promises of God. Promises that show me that no matter what my expectations are for my son or myself, God's expectations are even bigger and better.

His expectations for you are the same. So if you've left something undone—if something is hanging over your head in fearful expectation—don't wait another moment. Good things can come out of the darkness when God is the one leading the way. He has great expectations for you.

28

Silhouette People

Are you familiar with the popular silhouette art? Those pieces of black metal that have been cut to resemble anything from animals to people to places and things? Driving along in Kansas and Wyoming, I've spotted several of these. One was cut to resemble a wagon and an ox, another took the form of a buffalo, and still another was a stagecoach. From a distance on the highway, they looked fairly real. In fact, one silhouette caught my attention in Wyoming and caused me to believe it was the real deal.

There atop this dry, sage-covered hill stood the silhouette of a cowboy on horseback. From a distance, I was certain of what I saw. I figured some rancher was out for a ride and had climbed the hill to survey his kingdom. He had me fooled. As I drove closer, however, little things began to catch my attention. Neither the horse nor the cowboy was moving. There wasn't even so much as a flutter of the horse's tail in the breeze. Not only that, but as we approached, the proportions seemed a bit off and the size wasn't quite right.

When we drew abreast of the fixture, I could see that it was nothing more than a thin outline of the real thing. Just a silhouette to capture the imagination of what might have once been or of what could be.

That figure made me think of the times I'd dealt with other silhouettes. Only those were flesh-and-blood silhouettes. People who from far away looked like the real deal, but up close they were far from genuine. In fact, they were often one-dimensional.

For instance, I knew a woman who from a distance seemed like the real thing. She was bubbly and enthusiastic, portrayed an image of beauty and grace, and attempted to involve herself in good works. I drew closer as we were put side by side to work on something, and I began to realize there really wasn't much to her.

"Don't you love my hair?" she asked as we sat down to work. "I just think it's about as perfect as it can get. I wouldn't have worn it this way, but I've just lost twenty pounds, and I figured a body in this good a shape deserved a hairstyle to match."

I was rather hesitant with my comments. There was a part of me that wanted to agree just for the sake of avoiding a more in-depth discussion. But there was another part of me that thought the entire matter very sad. This woman obviously needed my affirmation, but I wasn't sure why.

Our time together continued to focus on her no matter how hard I tried to bring it back to the project. I ended up doing most of the work, while she took most of the credit. After the situation was wrapped up, someone came up to me and commented, "You ended up doing most of the work, didn't you?"

I looked at the woman questioningly, because I didn't want to cause problems for the other woman. But she understood my situation and added, "I've been teamed up with her before. So have many of the other women here. No one wanted to work with her again, so we figured, you were the new gal on the block, why not assign her to you?" She gave me a rather embarrassed smile and added, "She has good intentions, but there's no substance."

She was a silhouette person. She looked like the real thing at a distance. She was good-natured and kind, even willing. But there was nothing to back it up. She was as empty as a person could be without actually stepping out of her skin.

Maybe you know a silhouette person. I've worked with several in my life, and I'm still not very good at spotting them. If I were, I'd probably run screaming in the opposite direction, and God would probably rather I didn't. But silhouette people are hard to deal with.

Focused on themselves, because it's the only thing that gives them a semblance of existence, these folks are hard to understand. They aren't bad people, but they're needy, hurt others, and use others. They hope and dream, just like everyone does, but all those hopes and dreams are wrapped up in themselves.

"How does it apply to me?" or "What's in it for me?" are their life mottos.

Silhouette people aren't much use to anyone. While they look good from far away, up close they are found lacking. Spiritually speaking, there are a lot of silhouette people. I've been one myself.

You give the pretense of looking spiritual and holy. You carry your Bible, you go to church, you memorize churchaneze—those spiritual, pithy sayings we hear all around us.

"Well, the Lord laid this on my heart to share with you."

"I'm going to pray for your salvation."

"Here, let me quote you a verse from the Bible."

They have the right stance and verbiage, but they have no substance. When you draw close to them—when you need them for something—they often show themselves to be nothing more than the image of what you thought they were. Silhouette people might look nice, but they don't offer much beyond aesthetics.

The Bible gives us a view into the lives of people who were touched by Jesus. Jesus loved everyone, even the silhouette people. Maybe especially them. He knew about their emptiness. He knew that somewhere along the way, the world had corrupted their thinking and turned them away from real growth. He knew their hearts were fixed on themselves and that they might take more effort than any of the other people, but He knew that once some meat was put on those bones, they would flesh out and be useful.

Take the story of the Good Samaritan. Jesus is dealing with an expert in the law. The man is testing Jesus. From a distance, this man looks pretty good. He's knowledgeable, probably the type they call on when they need an answer to one of those pesky Torah problems. But he's also into himself—that much is clear—or he'd never draw that kind of attention to himself.

He questions Jesus. "Teacher," he asked, "what must I do to inherit eternal life?"

Now, Jesus was on to him. He knew the man was one of those silhouette people. In the tenth chapter of Luke, verse 26, Jesus replies, "What is written in the Law? How do you read it?" See, he knew that the law was the image of this silhouette.

The man answered, " 'Love the Lord your God with all your heart and with all your soul and with all your strength and with all your mind'; and, 'Love your neighbor as yourself.' "

He had it all memorized. That was his structure; the only basis for his substance was the law. A good start, maybe, but the man stopped there. He was absorbed in his pride of what he knew and thought to shame Jesus in front of everyone else by catching Him up in His answer.

But the story doesn't stop there. Jesus has hope for this silhouette man.

"Jesus replied, 'Do this and you will live.' "

Simple stuff, huh? Love God with everything you have, love each other as yourself. No problem, right?

Not so quick. The man wasn't satisfied.

"But he wanted to justify himself, so he asked Jesus, 'And who is my neighbor?' "

Jesus then breaks into the story about the man who went down from Jerusalem to Jericho. This man was beaten, robbed, and left for dead. A priest happens by, probably looking quite regal in his priestly garments. He had the appearance of being someone important, someone with value. But rather than help the dying man, he goes out of his way to the other side of the road. After all, he's a priest, and clean, and there were all sorts of implications to becoming dirty.

The next person on the scene is also a silhouette of goodness. He's a Levite. Oh boy. Talk about importance. He's of the tribe of

Levi, those appointed by the Lord back in Old Testament days to be in charge of the tabernacle and all its furnishings. They were the ones who were allowed to take care of God's dwelling place among the Israelites. Anyone else who touched the tabernacle furnishings would be put to death. The Levites set up their tents around the tabernacle rather than with everyone else, and they weren't counted along with the rest of the tribes of Israel. They were set apart.

The Levite also passes the dying man. The shadow of his silhouette probably didn't even touch the man's bleeding body.

At last we have the Samaritan—those folk hated by the Jews. They were looked down upon, scorned, considered to be totally unacceptable as company for anyone, but especially for the Jews. So what happens with this low-life scum of a man who isn't worthy to touch the sandals of a Jew?

Jesus is speaking: "When he saw him [the injured man] he took pity on him. He went to him and bandaged his wounds, pouring on oil and wine. Then he put the man on his own donkey, took him to an inn and took care of him. The next day he took out two silver coins and gave them to the innkeeper. 'Look after him,' he said, 'and when I return, I will reimburse you for any extra expense you may have.' "

This wasn't a silhouette man—this was God with skin on. A loving man, whose heart was full of the substance needed to make himself of real value to his fellow man.

Jesus asks the expert in the law, " 'Which of these three do you think was a neighbor to the man who fell into the hands of robbers?'

"The expert in the law replied, 'The one who had mercy on him.'

"Jesus told him, 'Go and do likewise' " (Luke 10:25–37).

I often wonder what happened to the silhouette expert in the law. Did he see what Jesus was saying? Did he understand that he needed more than to know the law? He needed to live the love of God before his neighbors. In the long run it wouldn't matter how well he knew the law, but rather whether or not he'd loved as Jesus had commanded.

I can relate to an expert in the law. Not because I'm an expert, because I'm not. No, I relate to him because there have been times when I was guilty of testing God—of throwing out my questions so that I could somehow find a loophole for what I wanted. Sometimes I'm nothing more than a spiritual silhouette—distracted by religion, the world, my friends, my family, or myself.

Sometimes I'm not the one kneeling to help bandage my bleeding neighbor, but rather I'm crossing the road, posthaste, to avoid having to acknowledge that he's bleeding in my walkway.

Who are you avoiding?

Better yet, why are you avoiding that person? Fear? Distaste? Time? Schedule? Disinterest?

Maybe from a distance you give the appearance of a generous person. Everyone is fairly sure of who and what you are, until they get next to you. Standing up close and personal, they find there is nothing but a shell—a silhouette.

"God with skin on" doesn't mean we become gods or that we take God's place. It means we let God fill us—work through us— permeate everything about us. As we draw on Him for nourishment, we fatten up. Our frame fills out, and we put flesh on the bones. But better still, we have real substance, and that substance is God himself. We become His ambassador. Not us in our strength, but God in His.

Fear may well have kept the priest or the Levite from helping the beaten man on the roadside. They might have been afraid of what would be required of them should they stop. Worse yet, it might have been a trick—an ambush that would cost them their own purses or lives. Then again, their schedules may have been pressed, and they wanted no part of something that would disrupt their day. Or, they could have simply not cared. Disinterested, they left the problem for someone else.

Their attitude might well have been "If I don't acknowledge him, he isn't really there." A good many people have that attitude. Many towns refuse to build homeless shelters, because if they don't build it—they won't come. At least that's the hope, but it's seldom the reality. If we close our eyes and plug our ears and walk on by, then we won't see or hear the unpleasant things that might require that we care. We can go on being silhouettes of what God intends us to be.

"But I don't have the time or the strength or the money to help," you might say. I know, because I've said those same things.

I've come to learn that God in us gives us the strength and ability to bear things we never thought we could bear. We can deal with uncomfortable people in our life. In fact, after a time we realize there aren't as many difficult people as we imagined. God has given us new eyes in which to see them and a new heart with which to love them. They aren't quite as unlovely or as unlovable as we once thought.

Who's bleeding on your street?

Maybe you find yourself face-to-face with the homeless. Perhaps teenagers or young adults who dress in gothic black and pierce their bodies are those you find in your path. Or the elderly with minds fading to Alzheimer's disease might be the wounded you go out of your way to avoid.

God in us allows us to bind up bleeding wounds, even if we used to faint at the sight of blood. He stands with us, even when we're afraid. He gives us power to face unpleasant situations, even dangerous ones: lions' dens and fiery furnaces.

Don't be a silhouette of what God wants you to be. People are dying right in front of you. They are beaten and stripped of everything. Will you walk on by?

29

The Storm Around Us

At the age of nineteen, our daughter Julie decided to take a long-distance trip with friends. We held great concern for her the entire time. She was driving a car that was less than reliable, and not one person in the group had much money. We prayed for her while she was gone, but I have to admit, I wasn't very good about letting go and letting God take care of the situation.

Parents never stop worrying about their child. They never stop caring, even when their child is an adult. Maybe especially when their child is an adult. It's hard to remember that God is in control even when you no longer are.

We weren't all that surprised when Julie called for help. They were on their way home, with nearly two hundred miles yet to go, when the car's engine blew. I was more than a little frustrated and a whole lot worried. I began to pray, not wanting my worry to absorb me, but my focus was on my child. I worried whether or not there would be good people to help her. I stewed and fretted over the image of my daughter being stranded in a strange place with no money for food or a place to stay.

We loaded up the car and headed out as quickly as we could. Bad weather had been forecast. Dangerous thunderstorms and high winds were possibilities. We lived in Kansas then, and the threat of tornadoes always accompanied those thunderstorms. But our child was in need, and the thought of her stranded in a strange town was more terrifying than the possible storm. This was especially true given all the horror stories on television that tell us about young women who have disappeared for seemingly no reason.

I continued to think about the situation all the way down Interstate 70 as we headed for Missouri. I knew my mind wasn't where it was supposed to be, but I kept telling God that Julie was my child, and I needed to know that she was safe and sound. I went back and forth between being angry that she'd taken the trip in the first place to being grateful that she'd felt comfortable enough to call us for help. I pleaded with God to make the time and distance pass more quickly so that we could see for ourselves that Julie was all right.

We arrived in the small town of Kingdom City, Missouri, to find the kids doing pretty well. They were burned out and tired from long hours on the road, but otherwise they were in good spirits. We took care of the car situation and then loaded the young people and their gear into our van. It was cramped quarters, for sure.

"We're going to have to hurry to get this all loaded before it starts to rain," I told them. Now that Julie was out of danger, I was looking to the skies. My husband concurred with this assessment, and everyone went to work double-time as the skies got darker and darker.

We hit the highway just as the first few drops of rain started to fall. I was driving and figured if the worst we had to endure was a steady downpour, I could handle it. But that wasn't the worst of it. As the skies churned in the distance, we knew we were heading into a nasty storm. There was no other direction to go. The way home was through that storm.

Sometimes in life we face a similar situation. We see the skies turn dark and hear the rumble of thunder: A child falls into bad company and makes some poor choices. We know we have to deal with it, but the horror of the storm is enough to make us want to turn back.

Or, the storm could be an abusive marriage. The threat of harm is great, and we have no choice but to drive head-on into gale-force winds.

Whatever the storm, the situation is never easy to face, and often the terror before us is all we can see. Our attention is so completely fixed on the circumstances that we forget there is a source of comfort to be had.

As the storm on I–70 closed in, we realized we needed to get off the road. The rain was coming down so hard we couldn't even see beyond the windshield. We were going to have to sit it out with nothing more than our vehicle for protection. My heart was doing a rapid staccato beat as the wind picked up and began to rock the car.

Then I began to pray through my anxiety. I would rather have been just about anyplace but where we were. The radio announcer advised everyone to take cover. In our neck of the woods, that's a pretty serious statement. If a storm like this had come up at home, we would have been safe in the basement, fairly at peace with the elements around us. But that wasn't an option. As the storm raged around us with lightning and thunder so loud we were sure it might shatter the windows, God taught me a very important lesson.

So long as I remained in the van, the storm wasn't really touching me. The wind howled and rocked the car, but it wasn't harming me. The rain and even a little hail assaulted the outside frame, but inside we were safe and dry. My spirit began to calm as I got a picture of my life. Storms might rage around me at any given time, for any number of reasons. They could come in the form of rains: an annoying deluge of bills or hurt feelings. They could build to terrifying thunderstorms: family illness or ugly arguments. There could even be an occasional tornado of devastating news: Grandma has Alzheimer's. A loved one has died of a heart attack. Good friends are getting a divorce.

Storms will rage, because that's the way life is. God's protection, however, is there for anyone who seeks it. He offers a refuge where we can ride out the storm. He only asks that we come to Him, that we stay with Him.

Had I opened the door and stepped out into the storm, I would have been overcome by the wind and the rain. I might even have been struck by lightning. I would no longer have the protection of the van. The same is true with the storms of life. Sometimes we step out into the middle of them, when we don't need to go beyond the shelter God has provided for us.

You might think it sounds pretty crazy that anyone would deliberately step out into a storm, but we do it all the time. We do it when we try to fix our children's lives. We do it when we demand our way in the middle of conflict only to create a bigger problem. We act first, without thought. We take our eyes off of God and put them onto the conditions around us, and the fear leaves us unable to sit still and ride out the storm.

The storm was never intended to be the focus of our attention. The storm is often the Enemy trying to distract us and steal our peace. God offers us refuge in the middle of our daily storms, no matter how big or small they are. But the choice of whether or not we accept the shelter is up to us. He doesn't impose His protection upon us. Instead, He shows us the contrast: how it is and how it can be.

There's a storm brewing in your life. Maybe it's off on the horizon, not yet close enough to define. Or maybe the storm is well within sight, but you've denied its existence. Each of us will have storms, but how we deal with them is up to us.

Your Father in heaven offers you protection: "He who dwells in the shelter of the Most High will rest in the shadow of the Almighty. I will say of the Lord, 'He is my refuge and my fortress, my God, in whom I trust' " (Psalm 91:1–2).

We need not fear the coming storm, because God offers us a shelter. Run to it and be safe.

That day in Missouri, the storm finally passed, and we were unharmed. We finished the drive home in a light rain, and the road was clear. Since that time, I've often remembered the truth I learned that day: Though storms may rage around us, we can choose to stay in the safe place.

God offers you shelter. He longs to give you a place of refuge and rest. No matter what you might see on the horizon, don't be afraid. God has opened the door to protection. Rest inside and wait out the storm. There's no need to be dampened by even the tiniest drop of rain. The storm can't touch you, if you stay inside with your Father.

30

Long-Distance Relationships

I don't believe God really cares," a friend opened a conversation with me one day. "He seems so distant—so far removed from me and my problems. I used to feel close to God," she admitted. "Now I feel like He's a million miles away."

Ever feel that way?

Have you ever felt like the only way to get through to God would be on a long-distance call, only you didn't have the correct change—or a calling card?

Have you ever looked up at the end of the day, riddled with problems and cares, only to feel certain that if you prayed you'd hear a message like "We're sorry, but this number has been disconnected."

One woman told me, "I can't seem to make my human relationships work right, and those people are right here beside me. How in the world am I supposed to make a relationship with God work when He's way up in heaven, and I'm way down here on earth?"

A long-distance relationship is how many people perceive a relationship with God. They joke about it: "Hello, this is the heavenly hot line. If you've called to talk to God about a problem, please press one." They rage about it: "If God really cares—if He were really here—He'd at least protect children from getting hurt." They cry about it: "Where are you, God? Why is this happening?"

God seems to live on some distant celestial shore that could never be bridged in a million years.

When I was twelve years old, I met Pam for the first time. Pam and I instantly clicked. We share many of the same likes and dislikes. I knew I would care about this girl for the rest of my life. I had great plans for how we would go to school together, grow up, and double date. We'd graduate and go off to college together and marry and have children and live next door to each other. At least that was the plan.

Then her military-obligated father was reassigned to an air force base in Alaska. That was about three thousand miles from Kansas, and it didn't bode well with my plans. Telling my friend Pam goodbye was the hardest thing I'd done in my twelve years. I was heartbroken, and it wasn't helped by well-meaning folk who told me I'd soon find a new friend.

Pam and I began a letter-writing campaign that crossed the years. We told each other everything. We grew up together on the pages of hastily scribbled notes. We talked about our dates, our mates, and our children. We helped each other with spiritual matters and lifted each other up when things were bad.

Once in a while we'd call long-distance, and in recent years we've enjoyed e-mail. In thirty years we've seen each other face-to-face only three times. The distance sometimes seems terribly far, and yet at other times it seems as if Pam were just next door. But always, always, I know she cares, and I know she's there for me.

How is it that we can believe in a friend who lives hundreds, even thousands of miles away, but we struggle to believe in a God who promised to come to us and reside with us—if we would simply ask Him to?

Our relationship with God can be so much more than our human friendships, and yet we seem to put Him on the back burner. Some folks see the relationship as a long-distance one. God lives way up there somewhere. He looks down affectionately at His children and from time to time gives them a warm, fuzzy feeling. Others believe in a more personal walk: a one-on-one through Jesus Christ that allows them to better understand their Father in heaven. They pray, read their Bibles, even fellowship with other believers, but when something goes wrong—really wrong—they get on the phone to their human friends, sometimes completely bypassing their best friend, Jesus.

Not long ago we moved to Montana, and in so doing, we left dear friends and family in Kansas. The distance is more than a day trip, and sometimes the separation seems tremendous. Yet we chose to make this journey, to endure the losses.

Sometimes we choose to distance ourselves from God as well. We know His love and comfort, we share in His goodness, and then we pull up stakes and head off for parts unknown. We know God is out there; we know how to get to Him, but we're focused on new territories and new adventures.

I call my friends from time to time. Sometimes out of need and frustration. Other times in joy and delight. I write to them and get letters in return. I know from firsthand experience as a twelve year old, that distance doesn't have to be a great enemy when it comes to friends.

But distance between God and us is always an enemy to our relationship. The distance allows us to forget. We forget the promises, the hopes, the responsibilities.

The distance makes us look to other things for comfort. When my friend Pam moved to Alaska, I tried to find comfort in television. When we move away from God, we often seek comfort in a variety of ways: people, places, or things. We may turn to comforting ourselves with buying lovely possessions, or to the influence of people and events. And all the while we feel isolated, homesick; and we never really understand why.

A youth leader I knew was fond of saying, "If you don't feel close to God . . . guess who moved?" And it's true. God is stable. He is real and sure and certain. He is steadfast. We are the ones who have a tendency to move around. Just one little step at a time puts us at quite a distance, and before we know it, we've made a major move away from our best and most trusted friend, Jesus.

Sometimes, sadly enough, it's only after moving away that we realize God was never very far at all. He was there with us the whole time. He was there when we lost our job, and we didn't know how we would ever meet that month's bills. He was there when the diagnosis was terminal, and the doctors all walked away. He was there when we needed Him the most, yet we somehow relegated Him to a faraway celestial home—available to us only through a long-distance service that had poor reception and outrageous prices.

When I don't feel close to my friends, I know either they chose to move away or I did.

When I don't feel close to God, I know who moved. I've only myself to blame.

The last chapter of Luke talks about Jesus appearing to His disciples after His resurrection. They still believe He's dead. They'd seen Him crucified and buried. "As they talked and discussed these things with each other, Jesus himself came up and walked along with them; but they were kept from recognizing him" (24:15–16).

Why didn't they recognize Him? Was it the grief, the confusion, or was it disbelief?

What keeps you from recognizing Him as He walks alongside you?

What lie has convinced you that a relationship with God requires a long-distance effort?

Jesus later chides these men for not understanding what He'd shared with them prior to His death. "Did not the Christ have to suffer these things and then enter his glory?" He asks in verse 26.

The group continues walking with Jesus. Yet they still don't realize the truth. It isn't until they are sitting together at a table and Jesus blesses the food and breaks the bread that their eyes are opened.

What will it take for you to realize the truth?

Jesus isn't a long-distance friend—out there somewhere. He came to you when you asked Him into your heart, and He's never gone away. Sometimes, just like with the disciples, He makes him-self very apparent. Other times, when we've chosen to move away, He waits patiently for us to send out the call. But always He is with us, even to the end of the age, just as He said He would be in the very last verse of the book of Matthew.

Does Jesus seem far away? Put down the phone. Put away that calling card. Open your eyes—the eyes of your heart—and call to Him. He's there right beside you, standing by. No busy signals. No long-distance operator needed.

I hear Him now. "Welcome back, beloved."

31

A Clearer Picture

I once had a teacher give me a good lesson on perspective. I had to close my eyes, and when I opened them again, she had placed a painting up close to my face. All I could really see were splotches and blobs of color. Nothing made much sense.

She pulled the painting back just a few inches and asked me what I saw. Again, it was mostly just colors with very little detail. I told her I saw green and blue and a bit of black, maybe brown. I couldn't make out a reasonable picture; none of it made sense.

She stepped back a bit farther, and now the painting was clearer. I could make out a lake and trees. Still farther, and I found the picture widening and becoming clearer. It was a landscape, which included a cabin by the lake, and behind it were mountains and a fading sun.

The object of the lesson was to teach us about expanding our vision to take in more than what was directly in front of us. She talked of going beyond the picture, to imagine our classroom and how someone looking in from the outside would see it. Children gathered around a table. One child stood at the front of the room. The teacher held up a painting. She challenged us to keep backing up.

Take it out of the building and imagine someone with the ability to see through walls. He would see the building and the landscape around it, but would also see the room, the children, the teacher, and the painting.

We kept going, imagining our town from overhead, our state, and then our country; then the world, and finally, the entire solar system.

I remembered that object lesson because the visual was so strong. I thought a great deal about how I often see nothing more than the blotches of color in front of me. I think I know what I'm looking at; I think I have a clear picture.

Then something comes into the scene to pull me back just a bit, and suddenly I realize there is more to the situation than I thought. The eyes of your heart can look at things the same way.

At first we see God through a glass darkly. We see the Word and try to understand and comprehend our little world through God's eyes. We see the blotches and the colors—sometimes we are so close to the canvas that all we see are tiny pixels of color—so small we can't even define their hue.

In Ephesians 1:18, Paul states his hope that the eyes of your heart be enlightened that you may know the hope to which God has called you. I have that same hope for you, which is why I've written this book. All around us, God is speaking in pictures that are vivid and powerful. Sometimes we catch a glimpse, and sometimes we don't. The sad thing is, often we don't even realize that we can't see what God intends for us to see.

When my daughter Julie first started school, we had no idea she might have a vision problem. It wasn't until she was tested that we learned she had astigmatisms in each eye. I felt horrible. I didn't realize my own child was struggling to see. To her, the vision she had seemed normal. She had always seen things with those eyes—those defective eyes. She thought she had a clear picture. I thought she had a clear picture.

Maybe you think you have a clear picture of what God is trying to show you. And maybe you really do. But there's also the possibility that you're still standing with the canvas only inches away from your eyes, and God wants to show you a bigger, clearer picture.

I'll never forget when Julie got her first pair of glasses. She put them on and stood amazed at the way they changed her world. I was delighted that things came into better focus for her, but my heart nearly broke later that night when we were outside. Looking up at the sky, I heard Julie gasp.

"Oh," she said in complete delight, "the stars! I didn't know you could see them!"

She'd heard us talk about the night skies. Heard others talk about the stars in the heavens. She'd colored pictures of five-pointed stars in coloring books. But she'd never seen them with her own eyes. She didn't know it was an option.

This book is written for all the Julies out there who don't know you can see with the eyes of your heart. It's for each and every person who is still standing with his or her nose against the canvas, longing to know what the picture is.

My prayer, like Paul's, is that the eyes of your heart may be enlightened. And for what purpose? Ephesians 1:18–19 says it all: "That you may know the hope to which he has called you, the riches of his glorious inheritance in the saints, and his incomparably great power for us who believe."

There's a whole view God longs to give us. He wants to put His loving touch on your eyes and show you that He is in the picture. He longs for you to know that He is in the everyday life you live— in the tiniest details. He desires for us to have a clearer picture of who He is and who we are in Him.

Open your eyes—the eyes of your heart—and look around you. I think you're in for a pleasant surprise, but I must add a word of caution. There is a price for this kind of sight.

Once the eyes of your heart are opened, once you see God in the details and understand the bigger picture, you'll never be content to go back to having your nose on the canvas. This kind of experience will change your life—forever.

Life-Changing Fiction by Tracie Peterson

Eyes of the Heart showed you how to see God in the everyday. Tracie Peterson's DESERT ROSES will strengthen your faith as you follow the stories of women searching for God's plan for their lives.

A Woman's Honor Meant Everything on the Frontier

For women of principle, the 1920's West was a difficult place to live alone. Becoming a Harvey Girl, though, made financial independence possible and surrounded women with friends and the wild beauty of an untamed country. But the Harvey Houses couldn't insulate these women from questionable suitors, scheming fathers, or the pain of loneliness. Discover how these women maintained their honor and grew in faith.

Delight Your Heart

Tracie shares her thoughts on why she writes fiction:

Fiction has always appealed to me as a form of entertainment and education; many of my favorite authors demonstrate that you can share a variety of information and still present a marvelous story as well. I like that about fiction. In my own writing, I love to take life experiences, both my own and those of historical characters, and mingle them into stories. The lessons God has taught me along the way are always useful to my writing ministry. And in blending all of these elements together, fiction writing seemed a likely format for sharing with others. Many people will avoid stepping into a church or picking up a Bible, but they will pick up a novel. When they do, I want my fiction to share the hope to which I've been called—that God has a plan for each person's life and that He loves us more than we can ever imagine. Writing, in any form, is a ministry I feel God has called me to. I want whatever I do to reflect my love for Him.

Tracie Peterson

Turn the page for a preview of Tracie Peterson's *Shadows of the Canyon*.

CHAPTER ONE

El Tovar Hotel, Grand Canyon, 1923

nd in here," Alexandria Keegan announced, "are the bulk refrigerator storage areas." Alex stepped past the new Harvey House recruit and opened the door to the unit. "We keep all manner of fresh produce, fish, and . . ." She fell silent as she heard the new girl gasp.

"Oh, Miss Keegan," the girl said, blushing red and turning away.

Alex couldn't imagine what the problem was, for the girl looked positively mortified. Turning to look into the unit, Alex fully expected to see a dead rat on the floor. Such a distasteful occurrence didn't happen often, but there was that rare occasion when something unpleasant marred the Harvey restaurant's otherwise impeccable reputation.

Alex grimaced at the scene. It was a rat, all right. But this rat was the two-legged type. Worse still, this rat was her father.

Rufus Keegan, well-known for his philandering ways, was at it once again. Pressed into a compromising position in the corner of the room, one of the newer Harvey Girls appeared to be enjoying Rufus Keegan's lack of discretion.

Alex felt her cheeks grow hot as embarrassment washed over her. How many times would she have to endure this shame upon her family? How could her father just go on humiliating her mother like this, never concerning himself with the pain he caused? Alex felt tears come to her eyes at the thought of all her mother had endured.

"Bernice, please go to the main dining room and bring Mrs. Godfrey." Alex steadied her emotions. She knew it would be better to have the dining room manager and housemother take charge of the situation.

Bernice, whose face was nearly as red as her bobbed hair, hurried off down the corridor. Alex turned to find her father smoothing the wrinkles in his clothing.

"Do you never tire of bringing shame to our family?" Alex asked, her voice a deadly calm.

"There needn't be any shame if you keep your mouth shut. Honestly, Alexandria, I don't see why you concern yourself with matters that have little to do with you."

Alex forced herself to remain silent and looked past her father to Melina Page. The girl was clearly embarrassed, but she didn't appear overly worried as she adjusted her black Harvey uniform.

"You should gather your things, Melina. I'm certain Mrs. Godfrey will have no further use for you," Alex said, staring hard at the girl.

"But you said you'd keep me from getting fired," Melina said, turning to Rufus. He only shrugged and chuckled. "But you promised!" Melina's voice raised an octave.

"He promised my mother a great many things, as well," Alex said. "But so far, he doesn't seem to honor any of those promises, either." Without conscience thought, Alex reached for the closest object—a plump, ripe, California tomato. "You are without a doubt everything the newspapers say about you and more. I'm ashamed to call you Father."

"Then don't. And don't take that tone with me. You don't have to call me Father or even acknowledge me as such, but I won't take a dressing down by the likes of you or anyone else. I don't take that tone of voice from the governor of this state! What makes you think I'll take it from my daughter?"

Shame was quickly overcome by anger, as years of betrayal seemed to culminate in this one act. Without warning, Alex threw the tomato. She picked up another tomato and then another. Hurling them mindlessly at her father, she shouted a tirade of disapproval.

"You don't care anything about my mother. You've caused her nothing but shame and anguish. Her health suffers because of you and she has no friends because you can't even give the pretense of discretion."

The ripe tomatoes splattered against the wall, against Melina's dress, and against the stun-faced Keegan.

Uncaring about the mess she was making or the vegetables she might destroy, Alex only knew that she wanted to hurt her father as badly as he'd hurt her mother. "We've suffered so much because of you. Mother can't even go to church for fear of what will be said to her!"

"Miss Keegan!"

The voice of Mrs. Godfrey caused Alex to pause. She looked momentarily at the confused woman, then picked up an apple. "My father and Melina chose to make this their trysting place." She hurled the apple, which her father barely managed to dodge before it hit the back wall with a dull thud.

Mrs. Godfrey reached out to Alex. Her grasp on Alex's left hand did nothing to waylay her from securing another apple with her right. This time she aimed for Melina.

"He doesn't deserve to get away with this." Alex nearly screamed the words, not caring who heard.

"Hey, what's happening? I heard the hollering going on all the way down the . . ."

Alex turned, catching sight of Luke Toland. The tall, lanky cowboy had his hat pushed back on his head, his sandy-colored hair hanging down over his left brow. He appeared shocked to say the least, but Alex could take no more of her father's indiscretion.

She jerked away from Mrs. Godfrey and reached again for the nearest object. It just happened to be a large stalk of celery. Before she could throw it, however, Luke stepped in and took hold of her.

"I don't know what's happening here, but I'm sure throwing this celery isn't going to remedy the matter." He spoke softly and eyed Alex with grave concern. His gentleness was her undoing, and her tears overflowed as she collapsed against his chest and began to cry.

"He doesn't care how much he hurts us," she sobbed.

"Miss Page, please pick up your apron and follow me," Mrs. Godfrey commanded. "Your services will no longer be required by the Fred Harvey Company."

"But Mr. Keegan said . . ."

Alex lifted her gaze as Mrs. Godfrey frowned disapprovingly. "It doesn't matter what Mr. Keegan said. You are in my charge, and we do not tolerate this kind of behavior."

Melina began to cry as she passed by Alex, apron in hand. "But I need this job. I—"

"You should have thought about that before you lowered your standards of decency," Mrs. Godfrey said, leading the weeping girl from the room and down the hall.

"Perhaps if everyone lowered their standards a bit," Rufus Keegan suggested in a loud voice, "we wouldn't find ourselves answering to uptight virgins and sour old biddies."

Alex twisted in Luke's arms and started to charge for her father, wanting only to scratch the smug look off his face and clean the air of his vile words. Luke held her tight, however, and no matter how she tried to fight his hold, her actions were futile.

"Alex," Luke whispered against her ear, "it won't do any good. He doesn't care."

Alex grew still in his arms. She looked over her shoulder, his face so close it nearly touched her own. Turning back to her father, she felt her rage further ignite at the expression on his face.

"I see this wrangler knows how to handle you. Good for you, son." Keegan smoothed the sides of his mustache and trailed the stroke down to his chin. "You know, maybe if you'd spend more time keeping hold of her, teaching her the more pertinent things of life," he grinned and approached Alex and Luke with confident strides, "she'd be a whole lot happier and maybe even more coop-erative." He paused as he passed by the couple. "See, I've always found that women were fairly easy to control so long as you handled them just right. Handle her with a tighter rein, cowboy. Show her who's the boss. It's about time she learned what the right man could do for her."

Alex drew back as though slapped. She could feel Luke tighten his hold on her arms, but it was the way Luke ground his teeth together that told her he'd reached his own limits with this conver-sation.

Reaching up to touch Luke's hand, Alex watched her father saunter down the hallway. "Like you said, Luke, he doesn't care."

"I want to put my fist through his face," Luke growled, his grasp becoming painful to Alex.

"You're hurting me, Luke," she said, patting his hand. He released her immediately. Alex turned and looked at her dearest friend in all the world. "Thanks for keeping me from making too big of a spectacle."

Luke's expression seemed to soften as he turned to look Alex in the face. "Your pitching arm needs some work," he said with a grin. Gone was the look of rage that had just been there. Alex could see his shoulders relax.

Turning back to look at the mess she'd created, Alex shook her head. "I couldn't help myself. I saw him doing those unspeakable things and shaming my mother, and all I wanted to do was hurt him." She looked back at Luke. "I wanted to hurt him like he was hurting me . . . hurting her."

Alex felt the tears smart her eyes again. "I try so hard to be a good Christian—to keep an attitude that would be pleasing to God—but then something like this happens. Oh, Luke, I can't take much more. How can I respect a man who so clearly does not deserve such honor? My mother has been hurt so much. What if she finds out what Father has done here today? Now her health has been suffering. I want to take her away from all of this, but she won't go."

"Why not?"

Alex shrugged. "She says she could never make it on her own—that Father would strip her of everything but the clothes on her back. She won't saddle her daughters with this, either. My sister, Audra, has offered to have Mother come live with her and her family in Wyoming, but Mother says it isn't right. But, Luke, it isn't right that she suffer this humiliation every time Father decides to chase after the newest Harvey Girl or hotel maid. It seems he's exhausted his possibilities in Williams, so now he's come here to the canyon and El Tovar. Soon there won't be a skirt in Arizona he hasn't tried to claim for his own. The management here is livid that Father would besmirch their good name."

"Why don't they forbid him entry?" Luke questioned. "After all, this is a luxury resort with plenty of important people. It's not like your father owns the place."

"No, but his political power and money keeps everyone hopping from here to Phoenix. He can pay off those who don't like his actions and cajole everyone else into doing things his way. Only the newspaper editor in Williams gives him a hard time, and that's because the owner has just as much clout as Father."

"I'm sorry, Alex."

She looked up at him, knowing he was sincere. He'd always treated her kindly in the four years since she'd come to work as a Harvey Girl at El Tovar. "I don't know what I'd do without you, Luke. Thank you for keeping me from making a complete fool of myself."

Luke grinned. "Need some help cleaning up?"

She shook her head. "No. I think the time alone will help me to cool off."

"That and closing the door," Luke motioned.

Alex had completely forgotten that they were allowing all the cold air to escape. "I should have never opened the door to begin with. Poor Bernice. She's the new girl. I was showing her around and . . . Well, the rest is pretty apparent. Anyway, I'd better get back to work. Seems like I'm always cleaning up my father's garbage."

"I really would be happy to help you. I'm done for the day and was just coming in to get a bite to eat." He seemed so eager to please her and the look on his face suggested a hopefulness that Alex couldn't ignore.

Alex patted his arm. "No. You've done more than anyone should have to do. Go eat your supper. You're a good friend, Luke." The look of pleasure left his face and was replaced with an expression of disappointment.

"Fine," he said and walked away without another word.

Alex shook her head at the hangdog manner in which he departed. Why should he be disappointed? She was saving him a great deal of messy work. Men! They were impossible to understand.